Stroke !

Stroke!

A Guide to Recreational Rowing

BRUCE C. BROWN

INTERNATIONAL MARINE PUBLISHING COMPANY
Camden, Maine

Published by International Marine Publishing Company

10 9 8 7 6 5 4 3

Library of Congress Cataloging in Publication Data

Brown, Bruce, 1945–
    Stroke: a guide to recreational rowing.

    Includes index.
    Bibliography: p. 140.
    1. Rowing.   I. Title.
GV791.B843   1986   797.1'23   85-31839
ISBN 0-87742-212-5

International Marine Publishing Company offers software for sale.
For information and a catalog, please contact TAB Software
Department, Blue Ridge Summit, PA 17294-0850.

Questions regarding the content of this book should be addressed to:

International Marine Publishing Company
Division of TAB Books, Inc.
P.O. Box 220
Camden, ME 04843

Typeset by The Key Word, Inc., Belchertown, MA
Printed by BookCrafters, Inc., Chelsea, MI
Illustrated by Larry Taugher

For Betsy, who gave me the encouragement, support, peace, and quiet I needed, all in the proper amounts.

Contents

Preface   *ix*

Acknowledgments   *xi*

Introduction   *1*

1   Recreational Boats
       —Which One Is Right For You?   *6*

2   Getting Started   *27*

3   The Perfect Rowing Stroke   *50*

4   Oars, Accessories, and Maintenance   *65*

5   Safety   *77*

6   Health and Rowing   *83*

7   Women and Rowing   *91*

8   Where Can Recreational Rowing Take You?   *95*

9   What It's Like Out There   *112*

Appendix 1 — Nutrition   *136*

Appendix 2 — Suggestions for
       Further Reading   *140*

Appendix 3 — Glossary   *142*

Index   *145*

Preface

Sculling is a strange sport, one of only two Olympic events that are done backwards (the other is the backstroke). It requires that you change your thinking patterns. You face the stern with your back toward the bow and your direction of travel. Your right hand is on the left side of the boat and vice versa. An equipment-oriented sport, sculling will still demand the utmost from your body. As you progress in the sport, you will be required to learn new skills and a new vocabulary. For all its strangeness and the mental and physical demands it will put on you, you will find it vastly rewarding.

There are two points I would like to make before you read this book. Like any sport, sculling has a large and specialized vocabulary. For instance, if you are using a pair of oars (as opposed to a single oar), they are not called oars, they are called sculls, and you are not rowing, you are sculling. In this book, I have chosen to use the more common terms, *oars* and *rowing*, interchangeably with the more correct *sculls* and *sculling*. I hope this doesn't offend too many purists. Secondly, I am neither a boatbuilder nor a designer, though I have studied both boatbuilding and design. My comments on construction and design are based on over 25 years' involvement in the sport. They are the observations of an oarsman, not an accredited designer or builder, and should not be construed as such.

To my way of thinking, rowing is the perfect sport. It keeps you physically and mentally fit while putting you in touch with a beautiful, clean environment. It offers a wide range of options for individual tastes and allows you to meet a diverse group of interesting, friendly people who share many values and interests. It is my hope that by reading this book and becoming involved in rowing, you will be able to experience some of the joys the sport has brought to me.

Bruce C. Brown
Laguna Beach, California
April 1985

Acknowledgments

Until you've written a book, you never know how many people become involved in the project and deserve thanks.

Betsy Zumwalt and Gordie Nash had the greatest influence on the content of this book. Along with sharing their knowledge of rowing, boats, and boatbuilding, they buttressed me with undying enthusiasm and contributed unstintingly of their time. Many segments of this book evolved from numerous discussions with them, but any inaccuracies are mine, not theirs.

Patricia Ingram contributed the appendix on nutrition.

Susan Livingston typed every word of this book and was always cheerful.

Larry Taugher created the fine drawings.

Phil Mason of International Marine was supportive and enthusiastic throughout the entire project.

Dave Pyle and Tom Ross introduced me to the glorious sport of rowing.

And, finally, I thank everyone I've rowed with over the last quarter of a century; I've learned something from every single one of you.

Introduction

Rowing has been with us since man learned the advantages of leverage and adapted them to movement through the water. Before then, boats had been propelled by paddles, poles, and rudimentary downwind sails. By devising a way to attach his paddle to a fulcrum point on the gunwale, man was able to use longer paddles (oars) for leverage in his stroke. By turning his back to the bow of his craft and bracing his feet, he could use both his arms and back, putting more energy into each stroke and producing more power. The combination of longer oars and added force permitted the development of larger boats, boats of a size that could not have been propelled by paddle or pole.

The honor of developing the rowed boat seems to belong to the Egyptians. The first recorded boat with oars appears in a relief on an ancient stone wall erected in that country sometime between 3300 B.C. and 3000 B.C. A very detailed relief from 2700 B.C. shows Pharaoh Sahure's seagoing war fleet. These Egyptian boats, which are known to have traveled as far afield as Syria, were equipped with both sails and oars.

For thousands of years, seaborne war, commerce, and exploration were powered by sail and oar. Ancient boats, which could not sail to weather or make way if there was no wind, relied heavily on oar power. The Phoenicians developed the bireme, a galley with oarsmen on two levels. By stacking their oarsmen, the Phoenicians concentrated more power in the same overall boat length and achieved greater speed. With the Greeks, the bireme evolved into the trireme, quadrireme, and quinquereme. Finally, with the number of oars at the maximum, the Greeks put more and more men on each oar.

History was shaped in part by oars and the men who pulled them. Cleopatra's barge was propelled by oars. Roman warships at the time of Christ relied on slave muscle at their oars. Viking long ships from the 10th century were powered more by oar than sail as they plundered Europe and explored the North Atlantic, discovering Iceland, Greenland, and North America. Saracen dromonds of the 12th century, English warships of the 13th century, and Venetian galleys of the 16th century still relied heavily on oar power.

Even though ships grew to such a size that oars could no longer effectively pull them through the water, rowing was not abandoned. Eighteenth-century corvettes, a class of warship slightly smaller than a frigate, frequently used oars as auxiliary power when all the canvas three masts could support could not find a breeze. At about the same time, whaling ships were putting oar-powered whaleboats to good use not just in the hunting and killing of whales, but as tugs to tow the mothership when there was no wind. Not even the most ardent proponent of rowing could consider any of this long history as falling under the heading of "recreational rowing." This form of rowing was hard work at best and, literally, slavery at its worst.

The first form of what could be considered recreational rowing appeared in the very early 18th century on the Thames. Bargemen of that English river raced their craft as an outgrowth of their occupation. For years they had been attempting to beat each other to paying customers; now they simply turned this activity into a sport, a sport on which betting thrived. In the early 19th century, English gentlemen came to the sport of rowing, and in 1829 the first Oxford-Cambridge Race was staged. The early races were rowed in boats similar to the barges of a century before. These were wide, heavy, planked craft with fixed seats and their oarlocks on the gunwales. In 1846, Oxford developed the outrigger, allowing their crew to mount their oarlocks outboard of the gunwale. This permitted a narrower, lighter hull, while still achieving the same leverage.

In 1852, the first Yale-Harvard Race was staged in boats similar to

These dories built at Mystic Seaport are faithful replicas of the boats that fished the Grand Banks. They are seaworthy, tough, and capable of carrying heavy loads. Such boats have rowed great distances in every imaginable kind of weather.

the English racing boats. It was Yale that out-teched the opposition In 1870, Yale oarsmen appeared with greased leather pants. With their feet locked in place, they slid back and forth on smooth wooden planks, incorporating the power of their legs into the rowing stroke. A year later, the rolling (now called the "sliding") seat was invented. The racing shell was complete—a narrow, easily driven hull; wide outriggers to spread the oarlocks; foot blocks to anchor the feet; and a sliding seat to allow every muscle in the body to drive the oars through the water.

To be sure, the design of the racing shell has changed over the hundred years since the first appearance of the sliding seat, but these changes have consisted of refinements and the introduction of new materials and construction techniques, rather than conceptual innovations. In the last century, the racing shell has become lighter, stiffer, narrower, and longer, all in the search for speed. It has been refined to the point that it does only one thing—go very fast in a straight line across smooth water. Through its evolution, the racing shell has become the preserve of the racing elite.

While the racing shell was being developed by collegiate oarsmen, another group was taking up rowing as a sport. In the late 19th century, more people found they had spare time for recreation, and many of them turned to boating. In England, a variety of gigs were rowed and raced for pleasure. In America, workboats, such as peapods, dories, and Whitehalls, were pressed into service as recreational craft. Over the years, these boats developed away from their utilitarian origins, and many became elegant pleasure craft. They did, however, retain many of the workboat attributes that had attracted people to them in the first place. They were seaworthy and strong, they could be rowed off beaches, and they did not require great care in handling. Unfortunately, they also had some drawbacks that made them less than perfect recreational craft. Though lighter than the original workboats, the new recreational craft were still quite heavy, and, with oarlocks on gunwales, they were wide and slow. Their fixed seats allowed the oarsmen to use only their arms and backs for power.

About 15 years ago, a naval architect by the name of Arthur Martin did a wonderful thing—he combined the sliding seat and outriggers of the racing shell with an easily driven though stable hull, and modern recreational rowing was born. Martin had recognized a need and filled it in a brilliant way, as Chapter 1 will describe.

Working both the heart and lungs, sliding-seat rowing is possibly the best aerobic exercise. While a rower's lungs process cubic yards of air and his heart pumps oxygen-rich blood through his body, sliding-seat rowing is also working every muscle of his legs, abdomen, chest, back, and arms. Unlike cycling, jogging, or walking, sculling is a "complete" workout. It makes demands upon the entire body and doesn't require any form of exercise to augment it. Shell rowers had known this for years.

Sliding-seat rowing burns about twice the calories of jogging in a given amount of time, and it is an injury-free sport. Oarsmen's knees don't give out on them, and they don't develop shin splints. Few, if any, rowers have been hit by a car or chased by a dog while practicing their sport. While scullers are getting their exercise, they are not

The first of the recreational rowing boats, the Martin Marine Alden Single, is 16 feet long and 25 inches wide, and weighs 65 pounds with its Oarmaster aboard. The boat pictured here is fitted with Martin's Feather Oars.

pounding their bodies with each stride, going on and off curbs, dodging traffic, or breathing foul exhaust fumes. Instead, they are gliding rhythmically on a nearly silent conveyance and enjoying the clean environment of water and air. When a rower finishes his daily workout, he is tired but refreshed, and usually wishes he could have rowed farther, rather than wishing he had stopped sooner. Many people seem to have to force themselves to participate in their chosen form of exercise and will grab at any excuse to take a day off. Rowers usually can hardly wait to get out on the water, and most feel cheated if they are forced to miss a day. The psychological and physiological benefits of recreational rowing cannot be overemphasized—it is the crème de la crème of sports.

Recreational Boats
—Which One Is Right For You?

In the past, selecting a rowing boat was a relatively easy matter. The choice was severely limited by what was available in the marketplace. There were flat-bottomed working skiffs; seaworthy dories and peapods; elegant traditional craft; or racing shells. Each craft had its advantages and drawbacks. While they were fine examples of various stages in the evolution of the rowing boat, they did not meet the needs of the average recreational rower.

That did not mean, however, that they were not used. For years, rowers made their selection from among these types of craft, and rowing for fun grew slowly. Flat-bottomed working skiffs, usually stable, slow, and heavy, served as a means of transportation inside harbors. These wonderful load carriers acted as tenders for both pleasure and commercial craft, and were used for short trips from dock to dock. Dories and peapods, evolving from their workboat origins, became the boat of choice for many traditional rowers. Like their predecessors, the fishing and lobster boats of the Northeast, the newer dories and pods were seaworthy craft that could carry great loads and still move well under a pair of oars.

The traditional pulling boats of the late 1800s, the Whitehalls and guide boats, were also popular, but they tended to be heavy and expensive and required a lot of maintenance. There was one other drawback—something all these boats lacked—and that was the sliding-seat arrangement of a true shell. To many, the performance and exercise supplied by the sliding seat were crucial, and if they couldn't have all that extra power, they just didn't want to row. Their only recourse was the racing shell. Unfortunately, this was the answer for only a very few. Shells were and still are prohibitively expensive. While fast, they are incredibly unstable and unforgiving, actively wanting to dump the oarsman for the least fault in style. They are lightly built and therefore fragile, and they require constant maintenance. Because they are designed to do only one thing— namely, travel 2,000 meters in a straight line over mirror-smooth water—the rower must adapt to them, not vice versa. A racing shell cannot be taken out on a choppy day for a quick row. True shells have always been and will probably always be the exclusive domain of a highly specialized racing elite.

For years, rowers compromised on what they really wanted. Many bought boats that didn't perform as desired, and the boats fell into disuse. Then Arthur Martin came upon the scene. His company, Martin Marine, began to produce boats more suited to the recreational rower. He combined modern material—lightweight, maintenance-free fiberglass—with innovative design to produce pleasing hulls, but this was not the real secret of his success. Most people feel his greatest contribution was the Oarmaster.

It was the Oarmaster that brought the joys of sliding-seat rowing to all those potential rowers sitting on the beach or straining to move heavy boats through the water with only arm power. For its time, the Oarmaster was a brilliant concept. Fashioned from aluminum and stainless steel, the rig is a complete, independent unit. It includes seat, tracks, riggers, and foot stretchers. All the stresses and strains of rowing are self-contained, isolated from the hull of the boat, which allowed Martin to build light hulls. Since they did not have to be stressed to take the rigging, the hulls could simply be envelopes designed to hold their shape and keep the water out.

The fact that the Oarmaster could be lifted in and out of the boats made portability to and from the water less of a problem than it had been in the past. Suddenly, trailers and boat rollers became obsolete. The Oarmaster was carried as a unit, and the boat was tucked under the oarsman's arm and carried separately. The Oarmaster fit in the trunk of a car, and the boat rested snugly on a roof

*A true racing shell.
These boats vary from
designer to designer,
but most are nearly 27
feet long with a 9½- to
10-inch beam, and
weigh under 30 pounds.
They are built solely
for speed over a straight-
line course in relatively
calm water.*

rack. This simplified, one-person portability made rowing more attractive to many and opened waterways previously thought to be inaccessible.

The Oarmaster's portability and ease of installation soon became obvious to many boat owners and builders, and Oarmasters began to turn up in traditional small craft. Dories and pods with Oarmasters mounted in them became a common sight. In fact, Martin Marine produces both a 16- and a 19-foot pod, the larger of the two being fitted with a pair of Oarmasters. Other builders began producing light hulls and mounting Oarmasters in them. Sliding-seat rowing for the masses had arrived.

Martin Marine and several other builders were well ensconced in the recreational boat market when the fitness craze hit America. As joggers injured themselves and turned to rowing as a safer, more thorough exercise program, others saw the market potential of recreational rowing, and new builders entered the marketplace. Many of these new entries were men who had long years of rowing experience and brought not only new blood but new ideas and construction methods to the industry. Today, there are literally dozens of modern, well-designed, well-built recreational boats available at bargain prices. Before the consumer can make a wise choice in this abundance of boats, he must do two things. He must learn something about the different boats being built and decide exactly what he expects his boat to do for him.

WHAT IS A RECREATIONAL BOAT?

Obviously, any boat rowed for sport, be it a 150-pound flat-bottomed workboat with peeling paint and 5-foot ash oars or a 30-pound Kevlar racing shell with 9-foot, 9-inch carbon fiber sculls, is a recreational rowing boat. For our purposes, we are going to limit the term "recreational rowing boat" to modern, sliding-seat pulling boats designed for use in open water by rowers of all abilities. The Appledore Pod and Stonington Pulling Boat would be at one end of the recreational boat spectrum, while the California Wherry and Vancouver 21 would be at the other. These boats, and all the boats that fall between them, are very different, but more on that later. For now, we are concerned with the features they have in common, the reasons they are all grouped as recreational rowing boats.

Taken as a whole, most of these modern recreational boats fall into two distinct categories: the racing shell look-alikes and the imitators of traditional craft. The shell look-alikes—the Laser, ARS, Vancouver 21, and many more—group together quite easily. Differences between them are great, but they look somewhat similar and make comparisons a simple matter. The copies of traditional craft are a much more diverse group. They range from 16-foot dories and peapods to the 22-foot Viking Whitehall. Then there are modern

A blend of traditional design and modern materials and thought is embodied in this 16-foot peapod design, which is molded in fiberglass and equipped with a sliding seat, outriggers, and 9-foot 9-inch sculls.

boats that do not fit into either category, such as the Row Cat, a catamaran with a sliding-seat rowing station; the On Board Rower, which converts a sailboard to a rowable craft; and the California Wherry, which bridges the gap between the two main groups. For now, we will look at the two major divisions and see how they compare with each other and to other types of boats.

THE RECREATIONAL ROWING BOAT SPECTRUM

Traditional rowing craft—dories, peapods, Whitehalls, guide boats, and their progenitors—are the first standard we must use when evaluating modern craft. The differences between these traditional craft and modern pulling boats are vast; construction and means of propulsion are the two major disparities, though there are many others. Traditional boats were constructed of wood and held together with nails and screws. Modern boats are molded; most are built from fiberglass, but a few are constructed using a wood-epoxy lamination technique (WEST) that combines the beauty and flotation of wood with the low weight and maintenance of fiberglass. Modern boats, whether built with fiberglass or the WEST System, are far lighter than their ancestors and require considerably less maintenance. As we have already discussed, the boats we are concerned with in this book all feature the sliding-seat and outrigger arrangement rather than the fixed thwart with oarlocks on gunwales that was standard in the traditional boats.

While the racing shell look-alikes are lean boats designed to move one or two scullers as quickly as they can row, the imitators of traditional craft usually combine their ancestors' load-carrying and rough-water ability with modern craftsmanship. The result can be the ideal boat for many rowers. Beautiful little seagoing craft like the Martin Appledore Pod and the Stonington Pulling Boat can be rowed offshore with confidence. They can carry hundreds of pounds of payload, either passengers or gear, making them the perfect craft for a day's fishing trip or a camp-cruising voyage. Many of these boats, like the craft they're patterned after, can be rigged to carry small working sails and are quick when sailed off the wind. This sailing ability can make the trip home a relaxing one after a day's rowing or fishing.

While the imitators of traditional boats do not have the raw speed of the shell look-alikes, some of them come very close. The 16-foot Appledore Pod and Stonington Pulling Boat are both nearly as quick as some of the entry-level shells. What many of them do sacrifice in straight-line speed, they more than make up for in their rough-water and load-carrying ability.

The rower today has a better selection at lower comparative prices than ever before. While a classic Whitehall with a bright-finish, wineglass transom is still one of the prettiest boats around, all but the most avid defender of traditional craft would be able to point out a multitude of reasons why she would not be the right boat for the recreational rower of the 1980s. Built in the traditional way, these boats are heavy and require considerable maintenance. Unless you are fortunate enough to have the skills, tools, and time necessary to build your own boat, you will have to find a builder of traditional craft, and then you will learn just how costly these boats are. Wood has become expensive, and the time it takes to build a traditional boat also costs. This time factor will also affect your delivery date. If you were to decide today that you wanted a replica of a Whitehall, a Swampscott dory, or any other traditional boat, delivery could conceivably be any time from four months to a year from the date you put down your money.

Conversely, modern boats, both shell look-alikes and copies of traditional boats, are built of modern materials to be light and practically maintenance-free. Mass-produced, they are relatively inexpensive and available almost immediately. Most of the boats produced today are off-the-shelf items. If your dealer doesn't have in stock the exact model or color you want, all it usually takes is a quick call to the builder, and your boat will be on a truck in a day or two.

If the heavy, relatively slow traditional dories, pods, and Whitehalls are at one end of the pulling boat spectrum, there is another genre that slips in between the traditional boats and their modern copies with sliding seats. This small group of boats consists of copies of the traditional boats with fixed thwarts and gunwale-mounted oarlocks. These boats, usually built of fiberglass with a modicum of wood trim, tend to be quite short and heavy. They range from 12 to 15 feet overall and can weigh between 120 and 150 pounds. Along with their weight, lack of waterline length prevents these boats from being terribly quick—but then, they were not designed to race. Lighter and demanding less maintenance than the boats they were patterned after, this genre of small boats could be classed as "elegant rowboats." They serve as yacht tenders and for quick trips around the harbor. Taken as a group, they are serviceable, maneuverable, and seaworthy. They are at the lower end of the performance and cost scales for modern pulling boats.

In terms of performance, the opposite of a traditional boat is a racing shell. True racing shells are to traditional rowing craft what Formula One Grand Prix racers are to heavy-duty pickup trucks. Each is designed to do a specific job and do it well, but they are hardly interchangeable. If all scullers wanted from their boats was speed, everyone would be rowing shells. There are, of course, trade-offs for all that speed, trade-offs that most people aren't willing to make. Shells are expensive. They are fragile, requiring very careful handling and nearly constant maintenance. They are unstable in the smoothest water and nearly unrowable in a seaway. The load-carrying capacity of a shell is nil; in fact, a lightweight shell can hardly support a heavy oarsman.

It is interesting that, while in most ways they are exact opposites, boats at either end of the pulling-boat spectrum share two features that make them unattractive to the average recreational rower: high cost and extensive maintenance requirements. The vast center of the spectrum—what we define for our purposes as true "recreational boats"—was empty until Arthur Martin introduced his Alden Single. With this boat available, rowers no longer had to choose between speed on the one hand and seaworthiness and load-carrying ability on the other. Introduced nearly 15 years ago, the Alden Single, with its Oarmaster rowing rig, is still the standard against which all recreational boats are measured.

This industry benchmark, while ingenious in concept, is quite simple in design. She is 16 feet long with a 2-foot, 1-inch beam (as with all the boats that will be discussed in this book, "beam" here refers to the beam of the hull, not the riggers; oarlock-to-oarlock measurement is generally standard throughout the industry at 60 inches plus or minus an inch or two). Lightly built of fiberglass, her hull weighs only 40 pounds. The Oarmaster, which is adjustable at the stretchers and the riggers to accommodate oarsmen of different heights, weighs in at 23 pounds. Assembled, the Alden Ocean Shell weighs only 63 pounds. Granted this is more than twice the weight of a true racing shell, but it is just a third to a quarter the weight of many traditional boats.

Though the industry standard, the Alden is not a perfect boat. She is quite wet when rowed in a chop, and her flat bottom tends to flex or "oilcan" in the same conditions. In flat water, her shortness hampers her speed, and many experienced rowers complain that the Oarmaster's riggers flex too much, leaching power from the stroke. On the other hand, her stability and maneuverability are great boons to the inexperienced oarsman. Her easily portable hull handles rough water easily, and she is quite affordable, less than half the price of either a custom-built traditional boat or a racing shell. Of course, the Alden's greatest gift to recreational rowers is the sliding seat. The proof of the Alden's success is twofold: not only is she the industry benchmark, but nearly 15 years after her introduction, she is still in great demand.

Comparing Speed and Stability

The Alden Ocean Shell should not be considered the bottom rung on the ladder of available recreational boats. Instead, she lies somewhere in the middle of the great array of boats on the market today. On pages 16 and 17 is a chart comparing recreational boats by their two most significant characteristics—speed and stability. This chart was prepared by Gordie Nash, who is eminently qualified to make these comparisons. Nash is the owner of Rowing Crafters in Sausalito, California, where he builds a wide variety of rowing boats and acts as a dealer for many nationally marketed recreational craft. A keen rower for many years, Gordie has rowed nearly every boat on the market and all the boats he rated on the chart. Rowing boats he has built himself and those designed and built by others, he has won his class in nearly every recreational race held on the West Coast. His enviable record includes a pair of class wins in the ultra-marathon of rowing, the 35-mile Catalina Island to Marina del Rey Regatta. On Gordie's chart, the Alden Single falls almost precisely in the center.

As Gordie describes the chart, "The chart starts with the flat-bottom work skiff at the upper left and the racing shell at the lower right. Alden is in the middle. All the boats to its right are faster and less stable, while all the boats to the left are slower, and most are more stable. Following the graph, stability and seaworthiness are portrayed from greatest at the top to lowest at the bottom. In general, a faster boat is also less stable. This is revealed by the downward slope of the plotted points. Experience shows us that faster boats are longer, thinner, and lighter, thus less stable and less seaworthy. There are exceptions."

Speed and stability are, of course, not the only criteria by which we judge pulling boats, but they are among the most significant. They are a great place to start the search for the rowing craft that most closely suits your needs. Looking at the chart, we see that the modern copies of the traditional boats, the Appledore Pod and the Stonington Pulling Boat, are slower but more seaworthy than the Alden Single. We also find that some of the new racing shell look-alikes fall to the left of the Alden. Two of these are the popular Laser Shell and Graham Mark I, both rated slower than the Alden. On the other hand, a boat that looks very much like the Laser, the Small Craft Warning, is rated equal in speed to the Alden and nearly as stable as the Appledore Pod. To the right of the Alden, we find boats such as the Seashell, ARS, and Vancouver 21, which trade off stability for greater speed.

Faster is not necessarily better, nor is stability the only answer. The trick for the prospective buyer is to balance the two. For most people, speed is fun; the faster you can push the boat through the water, the more fun it is. Stability, on the other hand, gives the rower the feeling of comfort and confidence. Stability is also related to seaworthiness, making the boat safer and more easily handled in rough conditions. A fast, stable boat is the ideal, but hard to find. If you plan to row only in sheltered harbors, the boats at the lower righthand corner of the chart would be ideal for you. If your plans are to row offshore in a variety of conditions, you would want to move back up the chart and to the left.

Weight, Length, and Ease of Rigging

Of course, there are other factors you must take into consideration before you buy your boat. Along with the prevailing conditions where you expect to row, there are logistical elements to be thoroughly thought through before the boat is purchased. Weight is more than a performance consideration; it is also a logistical one. Weight will decide whether or not the boat can be car-topped or if you will need a trailer. Weight will also be the deciding factor in whether the boat can be carried to the water or if a cart will be needed. Finally, weight will dictate whether or not you will be able to handle the boat alone.

Like weight, length is just as much a logistical factor as it is a performance one. Most people can find a convenient place to store a 16-foot Alden Single, but a 22½-foot ARS can be another matter. If you have to store your boat in an inconvenient location, it may inhibit your rowing. If your boat is too long to handle easily and too heavy for you to maneuver comfortably, the drill of getting it to and from the water may become too much of an effort, and the boat will fall into disuse.

Along with weight and length, the rigging can be a logistical consideration. Basically, there are two types of rigging, fixed and removable. In this instance, "removable" refers to self-contained units like Martin's Oarmaster and Graham's fiberglass unit. Fixed rigging can, of course, be removed, sometimes simply by loosening a pair of wing nuts, but more often the dismantling process is more involved. Being able to pull the entire rowing assembly out of the boat, as with an Oarmaster, can simplify storage and transportation because it diminishes the beam of the boat and lightens the hull. Many pulling boats share slip space with large sailing or power boats,

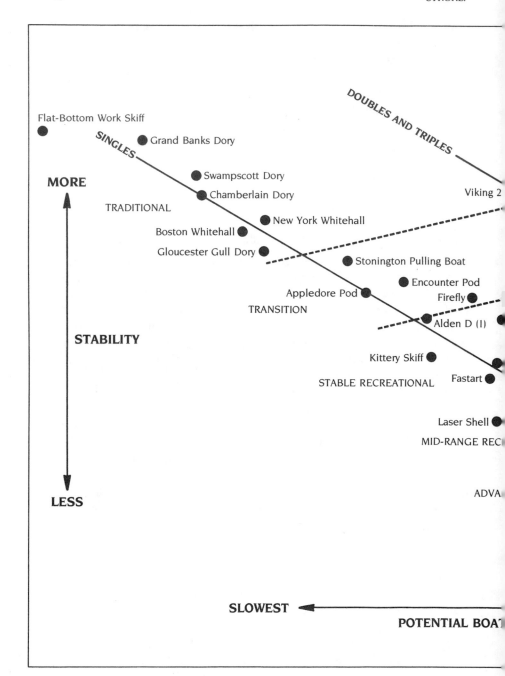

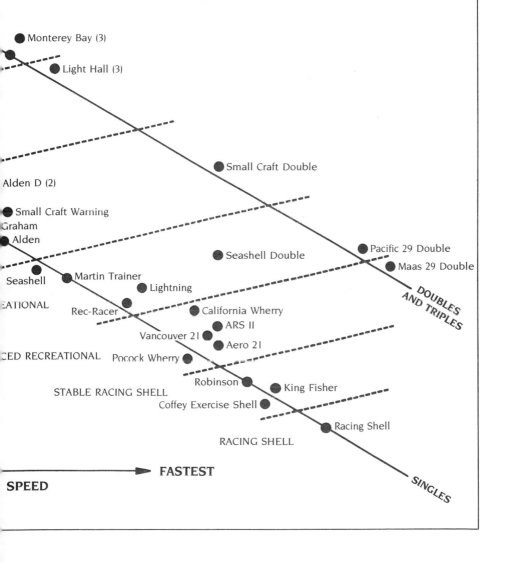

Comparative study of recreational rowing boats. Numbers in parentheses designate singles, doubles, and triples in ambiguous cases. The Monterey Bay (3) is a triple; the Alden D (1) is an Alden D rowed as a single. Note the seven regions of the chart corresponding to seven recreational rowing boat types from traditional to racing shell. (Courtesy Gordon Nash)

and being able to pull the rigging off easily can be a great help. Even if your boat shares garage space with the family station wagon, reducing the boat's width from 5 feet to 2 feet can be advantageous. The riggers of the Laser Shell are held in place by quick-release pins, while others can be modified simply by replacing lock nuts with wing nuts. On some boats, such a modification won't be as simple, and if overall beam is a consideration to you, these boats should be looked at very carefully. Being able to rig and unrig your boat with a minimum outlay of time and effort can make the prospect of going rowing that much more inviting.

Logistics are not as romantic a consideration as potential boat speed or the boat's ability to handle a pounding sea, but they are very real. No matter where your boat is kept, logistics will determine how much use you get out of it and how enjoyable it is. Human nature being what it is, the more difficult a boat is to get to and from the water, the less it will be used.

Capacity

Once the logistical considerations are well thought through, there are design factors to be examined. The capacity of a boat has little to do with its overall length. The Catalina 14, a 14-foot fiberglass Whitehall replica with a sliding seat, has much more carrying capacity than a 22-foot, 6-inch ARS, a shell look-alike. Capacity also means different things to different people. To some, it can mean the ability to carry wallet and car keys in a safe, dry place. To others, it can mean being able to transport sail bags and provisions from shore to a larger boat. Still others might see capacity as being able to accommodate a passenger or two and a picnic lunch. Whatever your definition, capacity will affect your choice of a boat and is a factor that deserves a great deal of thought.

To many scullers, an early-morning row is an experience to enjoy in solitude. It is a time to commune with nature, a period of quiet with which to begin the day. The prospect of sharing that time with someone else is unappealing. Others enjoy camaraderie and the very different challenge of rowing a double. These are also factors to be considered. If a double is attractive to you, but the thought of always having to find a partner to go out with on the water is not, there are convertible boats. It is important to note that a standard double cannot simply be rowed by a single sculler. The balance would be totally unacceptable. To row a double as a single, you must be able to reposition the rower's weight to balance the boat. The Alden Double can be rowed as a single simply by removing one of the Oarmasters and relocating the other. The same is true of the Appledore Pod.

Construction

Since many boats are purchased for their maintenance requirements, it will pay the prospective buyer to take a long, hard look at the construction of the boat he intends to buy before putting down any money. "Construction" does not just mean "finish." Most boats on the market today are beautifully finished; construction is another matter altogether. It refers to the quality of the workmanship and the selection of materials. The area where you row will make a difference in how you look at the construction of a boat. Some materials that will be acceptable in freshwater regions will deteriorate rapidly in the ocean.

Hull layup itself requires some inspection before you buy. A few builders, in their zeal to supply the lightest possible hull, have produced boats that are too flexible and might not stand up to hard use. In the same size range, you will find boats with hull layups that vary from a single layer each of 1-ounce mat and 10-ounce cloth, to two layers of 1½-ounce mat combined with two layers of 10-ounce cloth, or two layers of mat, 1½- and 1-ounce, and a layer of 10-ounce cloth. When you take a boat out for a test row, don't get carried away with the exhilaration of pulling through the water. Look at the hull, feel the boat; is it flexing or oilcanning? If it is, don't ignore the symptom—it won't go away.

While you're looking at the glass work, be sure to look for extra reinforcement at the riggers and in the ends. In areas requiring extra strength, some builders use foam, extra fiberglass cloth, or even carbon fiber. Others use nothing, ignoring the problem. Open inspection ports and look inside. Pretty gelcoat can hide a multitude of sins, so it is best to examine construction from the inside. If you have any doubts, ask questions. Talk to someone who owns a boat like the one you are considering and see if he has had any problems.

After you've convinced yourself that the hull is sound and strong, sight down it for fairness. You don't have to be a racer to get the advantages of a fair hull. Ripples in the hull or hills and valleys will slow the boat through the water, affect her ability to carry way, and make rowing her that much harder. Be sure the boat you are going to buy has a smooth, fair hull.

Decking is still another consideration. Most recreational boats have fiberglass decks, but some, such as the Scullcraft and Fastart 21, are open boats. Open boats, like shells, can be decked with thin sheet plastic (similar to garbage bag material), but this is not always satisfactory for rough-water rowing or the handling some recreational boats receive. If you are going to row regularly in open water, a stiff deck with sealed flotation compartments is recommended.

Boats with stiff decks have a joint between the hull and deck, and this requires inspection. On some boats, this is a rather narrow 90-degree flange on the underside of the deck just inboard of the edge. The deck is glued to the hull, and the flange is covered with a vinyl (or similar) rubrail to protect both the gelcoat and the joint. While the limited gluing surface doesn't seem to be a problem on these boats, the rubrail itself can be. Some builders glue the rail to the joint. This is far superior to simply heat-shrinking it in place. Of course, the attachment of the rubrail would probably not determine your decision to buy or not buy a boat. A heat-shrink rubrail that slips loose can easily be glued in place by the owner. But if the builder has skimped on this final touch, you might want to take a longer look at other, more vital areas.

A second method of dealing with the hull-deck joint is a rolled lip flange. Both Laser and Small Craft use this method, which consists of mating together wide rolled lips on both the hull and deck, thus providing extra bonding area and improved stiffness in the sheer. Builders who use the rolled flange method of hull-deck attachment don't install a rubrail on the edge, so owners will want to be careful they don't ding the exposed gelcoat.

After inspecting the hull construction, it will pay to take a good look at the rigging and engine bed. Riggers are constructed of stainless steel, aluminum, and fiberglass, but no matter what material is used, the same three factors are important: stiffness, adjustability, and attachment. A few strokes in a boat will tell you how stiff your riggers are. All recreational boats flex some; the question is how much. Many will allow the oarlocks to rise and fall a half-inch through the stroke, and most scullers accept this. Others will deflect as much as three

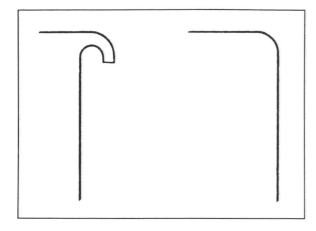

Hull-to-deck joints: rolled lip versus flush joint.

and most scullers accept this. Others will deflect as much as three inches fore and aft, and most experienced rowers find this unacceptable. The ability to change the height and pitch of the oarlocks can add greatly to performance and comfort. The Martin boats use nonadjustable bronze oarlocks, but they can be replaced with more tunable gated locks. Finally, the attachment points must be surveyed. If at all possible, find a used boat of the type you want to buy and carefully examine the glass around the mounting points. Have spider-web cracks started forming in the gelcoat? Has the glass deformed? Of course, either condition could have been caused by the owner's torquing the rigging while transporting the boat, or hitting a dock or buoy. If there's any question in your mind, ask before buying.

In the engine bed—that is, the sliding-seat assembly and the foot stretchers—most problems arise in the area of the stretchers. Beware the use of aluminum in the stretchers, especially if you are going to row in salt water. Being low in the boat, the stretchers are in contact with water far more than the sliding seat or the riggers. Rowed in choppy water, nearly all these boats take some spray over the side, and the stretchers can be awash constantly. Surprisingly, many builders use aluminum pop rivets instead of stainless steel in this vital area. Others use aluminum to build the stretchers or to anchor them. The structural aluminum is anodized, but often the threaded screw holes are not. These can corrode and capture a stainless bolt or screw as surely as if the hole was filled with Lock Tight. If your otherwise perfect boat comes with less than perfect stretchers, this doesn't mean you shouldn't buy it; simply be aware that there could be a problem later on, and be prepared for the extra maintenance required to keep the boat in top shape.

Safety

Like stability and construction, the built-in safety features you require in a new boat will depend to a great extent on where you plan to row. If you row in a harbor or on a small lake, safety is not as great a concern as it would be if you were making long offshore passages. All recreational boats have some built-in flotation—sealed air compartments, foam, air bags, or a combination of the three. None of these boats will sink like a stone if swamped. Some, however, will float considerably higher than others if they fill with water.

Most of the racing shell look-alikes feature a molded-in cockpit. This rather narrow, shallow indentation will simply not hold enough water, compared to the great area of air trapped in the ends, to sink the boat to her gunwales. Most of these boats are easy to bail while you sit in them and, in fact, can be rowed while the cockpit is flooded. Boats that don't have molded-in cockpits (the Graham Mark I and the Aldens, for example) can fill entirely with water. Their built-in

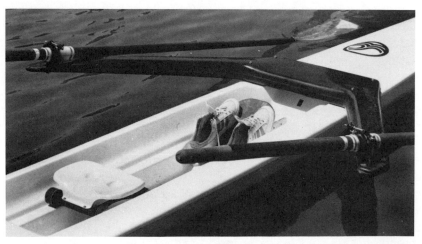

The cockpit of a recreational shell, an ARS, showing the new "wing" rigging and "super seat."

flotation will float them at the gunwales, but they will be more difficult to bail, and this should be kept in mind. Self-bailers can be installed in any of these boats, but the Elvstrom-style bailer functions only when the boat is in motion, and a Graham, when swamped to the gunwales, will be nearly impossible to get underway.

The copies of traditional boats are open craft and have large interior volume, volume that can hold great amounts of water. Most of these boats use either air compartments or foam for their flotation, and the effectiveness varies with both the builder and hull design. If there's any question in your mind, ask where the boat settles if she is swamped. If the design that fits your needs in other areas does not have the reserve flotation you feel is necessary, remember that air bags, foam, and air compartments can be added to many boats at a small cost.

How It Looks

After all the logistical and physical characteristics, there is the total package, that intangible known as "aesthetics," to be considered. To many people, a boat is not a boat unless it has some wood trim. Most

The cockpit of a true shell.

of these people will find the racing shell look-alikes disappointing. Many have wooden seats and wooden stretchers; everything else is fiberglass, stainless steel, or aluminum. Some don't even have wooden seats. More wood is found on the copies of traditional boats. There you will find wooden sheer rails, transoms, and (in the fixed seat boats) thwarts. Still others feature wooden decks supporting their sliding seats. If this is still not enough wood for you, both the Martin Marine Appledore Pod and the Hoban Kite Wherry are available in the WEST System. Looking like bright-finish wooden boats of yesteryear, these craft are eye-catchers wherever they're rowed. At any boat show or club regatta, the oohs and ahs are always loudest around the WEST System boats.

If wood is not your thing, then aesthetics is a matter of the boat's lines and colors. The racing shell look-alikes are available in a dazzling rainbow of hull and deck colors, many replete with bright graphics emphasizing shape or advertising the builder's logo. A boat is something to be proud of, and aesthetics cannot be ignored when making your choice. But remember, it is the design and craftsmanship that make a boat a joy to row, not the flash of bright gelcoat. When you're looking for a boat, look beneath the surface. A pleasing finish can enhance a good boat; it cannot make a poor boat row better.

Cost

Finally, one of the great deciding factors, not just with rowing boats but with nearly everything in our society, is cost. Recreational rowing singles cost in the neighborhood of $1,500. Doubles run $700 more. The singles' price range is actually from near $1,200 up to $1,800, and you can find a few a little lower and a few a lot higher. Quality and design are not necessarily factors of cost. If the $1,300 boat is right for you, you won't be upgrading yourself by buying a $1,700 craft. On the other hand, if you let price alone dictate your selection and you buy the wrong boat because it costs $200 less, it is no bargain. A boat that doesn't allow you to do what you want is worse than no boat at all, because it will be a frustrating experience.

Intended Use

Experts can teach you about design and construction. You can study Gordie's chart until you can put every boat in its proper place from memory. But none of this knowledge will do you any good until you know one more thing: what you expect from rowing. If you don't know what you want to get out of rowing, you won't have any idea what boat is right for you. If you want to spend a day once a week rowing offshore, possibly dragging a fishing line, you will not want to buy a Vancouver 21. On the other hand, if you want to use rowing as your exercise program and plan to do an hour to an hour and a half every day on flat water, you will probably want a more efficient boat than an Appledore Pod.

If racing is your aim, get to know the clubs you will race with before buying a boat. There are basically two types of clubs: the traditional clubs, which stage sprints for true racing shells, and the newer recreational clubs, which host races and cruises over open water. The boat one would buy for the traditional club would not be appropriate for the recreational club, and vice versa.

Before you buy a boat, you must also honestly consider your skill level. If you've rowed sliding seat, you'll have a pretty good idea of your ability. If you haven't sculled, most rowing clubs and many dealers give beginners' lessons. These lessons are a great boon to the neophyte. They will prevent your developing bad habits, introduce you to the basics of setting up a boat for the utmost efficiency and comfort, and allow you to row some different boats.

If you have sculling experience, whether you've picked it up on your own or just completed beginners' lessons, you'll want to try out as many different designs as you can before choosing a boat. Aside from being a learning experience, this can be a lot of fun. Dealers usually have more than one model, and they will be happy to let you compare them. Manufacturers frequently bring loaners to boat shows and are eager to have you row them. Trying out dealers' and manufacturers' demos may subject you to a barrage of sales talks, but it will be worth it. You will rise quickly on the learning curve. As you make the rounds of dealers and boat shows, and maybe row whatever boats are available at your local rowing club, you will meet other oarsmen. Most scullers will be happy to let you take their boats out for short trips and to talk at length about the features that led them to select their craft. These talks will probably be far more enlightening than the sales pitches of the dealers.

If you're new to sculling, with only the experience of a few lessons or a couple of hours in a boat borrowed from a friend, you don't have to limit yourself to entry-level boats. It would not be wise to try to handle a true racing shell after only a couple of hours in a very stable recreational craft, but with a certain amount of caution, a sculler with only a brief introduction to the sport can handle an ARS or Vancouver 21. The beginning oarsman will probably not be able to get the most out of these faster, less stable boats, but trying them out will certainly help him decide which boat is right for him.

As you row more and more boats, you will find that looks can be deceiving. Boats that look very similar can have very different performance characteristics. The subtleties of narrower beams and only slightly softer bilges can make one design faster, and less stable, than a near look-alike. Marginally lighter weight and a slightly longer waterline length, along with a few well-placed strands of carbon fiber for added stiffness, can also make one design faster than another.

If you were to walk the aisles of a boat show and look at the Laser Shell and the Small Craft Warning, you would think you were looking at virtually the same basic design. The Warning is 6 inches longer and 3 inches narrower, but out of the water these differences are hardly noticeable. A look at Gordie's chart will show you how these small differences, combined with some that are even harder to detect, make two similar boats such different performers. The chart shows the Warning to be considerably more stable and quite a bit faster than the Laser.

There are other examples of look-alike designs that turn out to be quite different once they are in the water. Many of the design differences that significantly affect performance are so minute only a naval architect or boatbuilder would be able to pick them out without rowing the boats in question. Fortunately, you don't have to be a designer or builder if you can row the boats. Subtle design differences become obvious as soon as you sit in the boat, strap your feet to the stretchers, and take one or two strokes. Even the neophyte sculler will be able to tell if one design is potentially faster than another, or if one boat is less stable than her look-alike.

If at all possible, try to keep an open mind during the selection process, and avoid locking yourself into preconceived ideas. Ask questions and try out new and different boats. Gordie Nash's well-thought-out chart is a useful tool, but don't depend on the chart as the total answer. It's easy and comfortable to make decisions from the advice of experts, but remember it will be you who moves the boat to and from the water, and it will be your body that drives the boat through the water. Trust your feelings about boats, even if you are new to sculling. If you feel good about a boat, if it feels right for you, it probably is.

Getting Started

Once you've chosen a boat, you're on your way to lifelong involvement in a wonderful sport. If you're like most people, you're going to want to take your new toy out and play with it as soon as it arrives. There are, however, a few details that will have to be attended to, and dealing with these before you try to row will make your introduction to the sport far less traumatic.

TRANSPORTING THE BOAT

The first obstacle you may have to overcome is the logistical one of getting your new acquisition to the water. Fortunately, automobile roof racks have improved greatly in the past few years. New racks are tougher and more efficient than their antecedents, and the dealer from whom you bought the boat can probably steer you toward the best one for you. If you decide to make your own choice, be sure to err on the side of caution, both in the rated carrying capacity of the rack and in its construction. Although a recreational boat may not be particularly heavy, it does have a lot of surface area and offers considerably more wind resistance than, say, a surfboard or a bicycle. Remember also that your boat will be wet and sandy, so buy a rack with a tough coating that will resist corrosion.

A very good way to transport a recreational boat. It is strapped down in four places, and thick padding protects the hull from the racks. A large red flag marks the stern. The gates of the oarlocks have been closed for the trip, and the seat has been removed. Note the padded covers on the scull blades. This rig is legal in California, both the front and rear overhangs being six inches within the maximum allowed. Overhang restrictions may vary from state to state.

Once you have the rack, install it with the maximum possible spread, so that the boat is well balanced and stable. Most recreational boats will overhang most cars both front and rear. To avoid any problems in this area, and since vehicle code regulations vary from state to state, read a drivers' handbook or consult your local automobile club or a policeman about how much overhang is allowable. There are a lot of misconceptions about these laws, so it is a good idea to get your information from a reliable source. You'll also need an exact description of what is required to mark the rear of the boat while it is on your car. If a red flag is mandated, how big does it have to be? If a light is required, what is the minimum wattage?

The design of your boat will dictate how you carry it on the rack. If she has the flat bottom of a Laser or a Warning, you can carry her upright. This relieves you of the inconvenience of having to turn her over when loading and unloading her. If she has a rounded bottom, like a Pocock Wherry, it will be best to carry her upside down.

The Latanzo seat, which is provided with the majority of recreational boats, has a pair of keepers that hold it on the tracks while you're in the boat or moving her about on the beach or dock. These keepers should not be relied upon to keep the seat secure while the boat is on your car. You will want to make sure that anything loose in the boat, such as a bailer, is removed before transporting. If your boat has a skeg, or fin, be sure it won't vibrate loose when it's on a car. Transporting a recreational boat can expose the craft to more damage than it would ever experience on the water; a little extra time and caution are well spent.

When you strap your boat to the rack, again, err on the side of caution. If there's any doubt in your mind that the boat is tied down securely enough, don't chance it—add another rope or strap. Each time you load the boat, the rack should be checked to see that it hasn't vibrated loose. This takes just seconds, but it can be as vital as strapping down the boat.

Some people might think using a trailer is easier than car-topping, especially for a larger boat such as an Encounter or Appledore, but this really isn't such a good idea. Trailers, especially small trailers, are not as well sprung as a car. The vibration and bouncing they cause can destroy a lightly built recreational boat.

Although they are light, recreational boats—like anything 18 to 23 feet long and 5 feet wide—can be awkward and intimidating to try to maneuver alone. Most scullers find it advantageous to either buy or build a cart to move their boat from a car or boathouse to the water. A variety of carts designed for sailing dinghies is on the market today, and most work well with recreational boats. If one of these doesn't meet your needs, commercially available wheels and axles can be mated to some 2 x 4s, with carpeting added for padding. Either way, a suitable cart can make life much easier.

While making plans for moving your boat, give some consideration to the sculls. Whether you've chosen carbon fiber or wooden oars, the blades are susceptible to damage. A pair of padded covers can prevent chipping and splintering. You can either buy these or have them made by a local canvas shop. When you hand-carry your sculls, always keep the blades forward; you will be less likely to knock them against something this way.

TUNING UP

If your dealer is really involved in recreational rowing rather than just handling the boats as a sideline, you can expect him to help you set the boat up when you take delivery. If he can't help, the coach or rowing coordinator of the local rowing club can, and if there is no local club, you and a friend can do the setup yourselves. It is important that *someone* tune the boat properly before you try to row it. If the boat is

A cart makes transporting a heavier recreational rowing boat a simple matter.

"fresh out of the box," chances are it's nowhere near being set up the way it should be, and if it has been around the shop for a while, you can be sure it isn't tuned for you, though it may have been rowed by a dozen people. Your natural inclination will be to take the boat out and row it anyway. Fight this urge. Unless the boat is properly set up for you, trying to row is going to be frustrating at best.

Oarlocks

The first components you will have to tune are your oarlocks. They must be set for height, pitch, and, in some cases, spread. The height will need to be set first. Oarlock height refers to the distance between the horn (the highest portion) of the seat and the bottom of the oarlock's inside surface. The easiest way to measure this is to lay an oar on its flat across the gunwales. Measure from the horn to the flat of the oar, then go out the riggers to either oarlock and measure from the low inside surface of the lock to the flat of the oar. The sum of these two measurements is the oarlock height. Your dealer or owner's manual should tell you the best way to adjust the height on your boat. It can be done by shimming the riggers where they attach to the hull, by placing a spacer between the oarlock and the oarlock plate or sill, or by bending the sill itself.

Since the handles of your sculls will overlap in the middle of both your pull-through and recovery, you will be rowing with one hand over the other. In the United States, it is standard practice to row left over right, so this is the way your boat should be set up. That way it will be easy for you to move from your boat to someone else's without having to adapt your style. For this reason, you will want your lefthand (starboard side) oarlock a half-inch higher than the righthand (port side) lock. If there is not enough clearance and you are forced to compensate by lowering your right hand, the boat will list to port. If there is even less clearance and you have to row with your hands level—say, left in front of right—it will cut the arc of your right oar short, and you will constantly steer to port.

If you are a person of average size, the height of your lefthand oarlock should be 6 inches, and your righthand lock, 5½ inches. If you are heavier than average, they should both be a little higher; conversely, if you are lighter than normal, they should both be a little lower. When you get in the boat, you will check the height by setting yourself at the release position with the blades, not the shafts, just buried in the water. Your hands should come to your body just below the chest, this being the most efficient release position in terms of using your muscles.

The next adjustment to be made is the pitch of your oarlocks. Pitch is the sum of the inclines forward or aft from the vertical of the flat

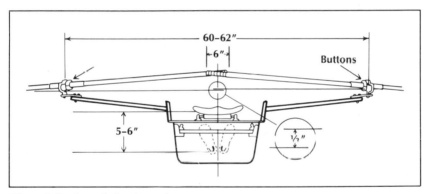

The cockpit, viewer facing forward.

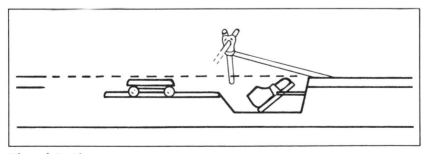

The cockpit, side view.

*Christian Maas rowing one of his Aeros. Note that his left hand has just passed
over his right.*

surface of the oar shaft and the vertical surface of the oarlock, which
the shaft presses against. If the vertical surface of the oarlock is
perpendicular to the surface of the water (that is, if it's absolutely
vertical), this is expressed as zero degrees of pitch. Recreational oars
have no pitch built into them, but many racing oars do. Therefore, it is
wise to check your oars for pitch before adjusting the oarlocks. To do
this, rest the flat, at the collar, on a level surface, with the blade
cupped upward. Then place a level across the blade. If it is level, the
oar has zero degrees of pitch. If the oar does have some built-in pitch,
you will have to keep that in mind when you pitch the oarlocks. You
will also have to mark the oars so they always end up on the same side
of the boat, each one in the oarlock that has been pitched to be
compatible with it. Oars with no pitch will be easier to work with, so if
you order oars, be sure to specify that they be built with no pitch.

   Setting the pitch is one way a dealer can really help you. Most
dealers have pitch gauges, and the job is much easier if one is
available. Whoever pitches your locks—your dealer, your rowing
coach, or the guy on the beach who knows the most about rowing—

should be asked to explain the process, because you'll want to be able to check and adjust your own pitch as time passes. If your dealer doesn't know what you're talking about when you ask him about oarlock pitch, and there's no rowing club, and you haven't met the local guru yet, you'll have to buy a pitch gauge or use a triangle and a protractor to do the job. A pitch gauge is better.

The Latanzo gated oarlock has become the standard for recreational boats, so that's what we'll concentrate on here. If you've purchased one of Arthur Martin's boats, or any other boat that comes with an Oarmaster rig, the brass oarlocks supplied with it cannot be adjusted for pitch. On the other hand, they can easily be removed and replaced with Latanzos.

To set the pitch, level the boat and turn your oarlocks to the proper rowing position—that is, with the body of the lock abaft the pin. You will first have to check for any existing pitch. If the oarlock faces already have some positive pitch, their tops angle toward the stern, and you will have to take that into account in your adjustments. If the tops of the faces angle toward the bow, the locks have a negative pitch, and this must be taken out before the proper positive pitch can be set.

There are several ways to change the pitch. A tiny shim can be added between the oarlock retaining nut and the sill; the stainless steel pin upon which the oarlock pivots can be bent; or the riggers can be bent, as can the sill. If you use any of the bending techniques, be careful you don't put in so much torque that you place an unnatural strain on the boat. Before bending the pin, take the nut off its top and remove the oarlock. The oarlock must be replaced to measure the number of degrees of pitch you've induced. Always measure off the oarlock, not the pin, because it's the oarlock that the oar contacts.

While it's time-consuming and maybe a little intimidating to set your own pitch the first time out, the task should not be ignored. Pitch affects the angle of the blade as it enters the water. If you put the blade in the water exactly vertically—that is, with zero degrees of pitch in the lock and the oar—the blade will not bite the water. It will knife in and dig deep, burying the shaft. To prevent this, you are going to need some positive pitch. The best way to see this pitch is to place the oar in the oarlock as if you were rowing. With the flat of the oar against the pressure plate of the oarlock, the upper edge of the blade will be tilting slightly toward the stern.

For the beginning rower, 6 degrees of positive pitch will be correct.

The more positive pitch you have, the less efficient your feathering must be and the less clean your blade work. The more proficient you become, the more you can decrease the pitch. Eventually, you will take your pitch down to 3 degrees. This will make it easier to keep your blades in the water, but you can only do this as you become more efficient—perhaps by the end of the second month of rowing. If you take the pitch down too soon, you will find your oars digging too deep.

Another adjustment you'll want to make if possible is oarlock spread, the measurement from the center of the starboard pin to the port-side pin. On many recreational boats, this adjustment cannot be made because the pins are set, but on some boats there is a modicum of movement provided. The spread should be 60 to 61 inches, assuming you are using recreational sculls that measure 9 feet, 9 inches. If your spread can be adjusted, it is important that it be set evenly on both sides. Therefore, you will have to measure not only the distance from pin to pin, but from each pin to the centerline of the boat. If the distance from the starboard pin to the centerline is 30¾ inches and that from the port pin to the centerline is 30¼ inches, the discrepancy will throw off your arcs, make one arm work harder than the other, disrupt your balance, and make steering a straight course almost impossible.

You'll need to make one final adjustment to your Latanzo locks. On the gate there are three nuts: a large locking nut with a knurled plastic grip, and two smaller brass nuts. The large nut locks the gate in place, and the two smaller nuts set the width of the gate by acting as an inner stop against which the trailing upright of the oarlock rests. The stopping nuts may be set so near the hinge of the gate that the oarlock is too tight to allow the oar to pivot from drive to feather position. Place each oar in the oarlocks and see that it rolls freely, not sloppily, from drive to feather and back again.

The Oars

Turn your attention now to the oars themselves. The oars will have arrived with the sleeves (the plastic sheaths that rotate inside the oarlock) in place, but more than likely the collars, or buttons, will have come taped together, dangling from one of the sculls. The buttons should be installed with the larger of the two cheeks facing the blade of the oar. This surface will rest against the inboard surface of the oarlock. It is vitally important that the buttons be set at exactly the same distance from the handle on each oar; if they are not, one oar will traverse a greater arc through the water, constantly steering you away from that side. The easiest way to check their evenness is to stand the oars on their handles side by side on a flat surface and make sure the buttons touch. If they miss by an eighth of an inch, take the time to realign them—it is that important.

The first time you set the buttons, set them so the oar handles overlap 6 inches; this will place one of your hands directly above the other. This setting may change as you become more proficient, but it's a good place to start. The less overlap you have, the farther from the boat the blades will be when they enter the water and make their pull-through. This gives you a greater arc, which is good, up to a point.

The law of diminishing returns is applicable to a large arc. Depending upon your own size and strength, it can become too difficult to move the boat with an excessively large arc. If the boat gets too heavy—if you feel that you're lifting weights each time you move it—move the buttons toward the blades. This will lighten the load by producing a shorter arc. It will also result in more overlap, but in time you will get used to this.

When you adjust the buttons, do so in small increments, never more than a quarter-inch at a time. A quarter-inch per oar will result in a half-inch difference in overlap, but more important, it will make a significant difference in the arc the blade travels through the water.

The sleeves will require lubrication where they contact the oarlocks. In the old days, sleeves were made from leather and required liberal amounts of grease to roll smoothly in the oarlocks. The days of leather are gone, and, thankfully, so are the days of slathering Crisco on oars. Large amounts of grease are messy and attract grit, which wears on the lock, sleeve, and button. When you lubricate your sleeves, use one of the new silicone or Teflon-based spray lubricants, and use it sparingly.

Foot-Stretcher Placement

The last component requiring attention is the foot stretchers. Their proper location will greatly enhance the quality of your sculling. To set up the stretchers for the first time, you must be aware of your body type. If you are tall, the stretchers will be nearer the stern; if you are short, they will be nearer the bow. If your legs are longer or shorter than normal for your height, you will want to adjust the stretchers accordingly.

The importance of foot-stretcher placement cannot be over-emphasized. It makes a big difference to your comfort. If they are too far aft, you will be cramped over the oars and will get the handles caught in your clothes or against your body. If they are too far forward, you can't pull your arms in, which makes you shorten your stroke and feel less secure.

You can check foot-stretcher placement before you launch the boat, and this is easier than checking it on the water if you've never been in the boat before. It will give you one less thing to deal with once you're afloat and will prevent your having to beach the boat to correct the location. If your boat has a fin, be sure to remove it before you set the boat on the beach or dock. The first time you put the seat in your boat, be sure the horn, the highest portion, is toward the stern, and the cutout for your coccyx is toward the bow. To check foot-stretcher placement, assume the layback position, as if the blades were buried in the water, with your arms pulled in. They should be in a natural position, hands in front of the body. They should not be pulled past your body to your sides. Be sure your shoulders are relaxed and your elbows are down. Then take your thumbs off the ends of the oars and point them toward your body. The tips of the thumbs should just graze your skin. Don't lean back to get the extra space, and don't adjust your body to the stretchers: adjust the stretchers to your body—that's what they're there for.

BOARDING

While you have the boat set up on the beach or dock is a good time to practice different ways of getting aboard and back ashore. Beach launching is easier than launching from a dock, so go off a beach if possible, at least on your first time out. There are three ways to board a recreational boat from the beach, but all rely on the oars for stability. To get stability from the oars, place them in their locks and square them to the hull. Be sure that the blades are cupped upward and that the buttons are firmly pressed against the locks. Grasp the handles together and raise them slightly; this will bring the backs of the blades in contact with the water and provide stability.

The easiest and safest way to board is to stabilize the boat with the oars, step in with one foot, sit on the seat, then bring your other foot aboard. To get out, reverse the process. Another way to board is to straddle the boat (assuming it is narrow enough), stabilize the boat with the oars, sit down in the seat, and bring your legs aboard. Again, to get out, reverse the process.

The most difficult method is also the best training for boarding a true racing shell. When you've just purchased your first recreational boat, it may be hard to imagine yourself boarding a tippy, fragile shell, but the day may come, and you should at least know the drill. First, make sure the seat is all the way forward, then stabilize the boat with the oars, but hold the grips together with only the water-side hand. The shore-side hand will grasp the riggers on the near side. With the boat stable, step onto the seat deck (the area between the seat tracks) with your water-side foot, and simultaneously lift the rigger with your shore-side hand to balance the boat. Draw your shore-side leg into the boat and directly to the foot stretchers. Still holding the oars and the rigger, bend the leg on the seat deck and lower yourself into the seat. The outstretched leg in the foot stretcher will help balance you so you don't fall quickly. Then extend the water-side leg to the foot stretchers. This will seem awkward and unbalanced at first. It may very well not be the way you choose to board the boat when you are new to it, but practice will make you comfortable with this method, and it is a good skill to master. Getting out of the boat is practically the reverse. With the oars stabilizing the boat, slide the seat forward to the release position. Raise the water-side knee, drawing the foot up to the seat deck. If you are stiff, you may have to use your shore-side hand to grasp the ankle and pull the foot in close to you. Then hold the shore-side rigger with your shore-side hand and raise yourself on your water-side leg. Pull the shore-side foot out of the stretcher and swing the leg over the side of the boat and into the water. Take your weight with the leg in the water and step out of the boat.

If you must board the boat from a dock, place the boat alongside the dock with the near rigger extending over it. Place the dock-side oar in its lock with the blade resting on the dock, then slide the water-side oar into its lock. To lock the water-side oarlock, hold the dock-

Getting into the boat. Be sure to pull up on the rigger; be sure the blades are flat on the water; and be sure to step into the center of the boat.

Getting out of the boat.

side oarlock captive against the dock with one hand, crouch to keep your center of gravity low, and place one foot on the seat deck. Then reach out with your other arm to lock the gate. Both oars should be in the stabilizing position, square to the hull, with blades cupped up. The seat should be all the way forward on the tracks. Hold the oar handles with the water-side hand and the dock-side rigger with the dock-side hand. With the water-side foot, step onto the seat deck, then give a gentle push with the dock-side leg and swing it aboard, directly to the stretcher. The push will send the boat slowly away from the dock. As soon as you've eased yourself down into the seat, put both hands on the oars and depress the handle of the dock-side oar slightly. This will lift the blade off the dock and prevent it from scraping. As soon as that blade is clear of the dock, lower it to the surface of the water. Getting back onto the dock is practically the reverse, but requires some skilled boat handling while coming alongside.

YOUR FIRST ROW

Once the boat is roughly tuned and you've decided how you are going to board her, it is time, at last, to introduce her to her natural environment, the water. If it's at all possible, choose a small, protected cove for your first outing. This will give you a more secure feeling than if you were in open water. You also should choose a calm day, and even if there isn't a breath of wind or an inch of chop, launch as if conditions were less than favorable. It will stand you in good stead later on.

You will want to be able to get away from the beach as soon as possible if there is wind or chop, especially an onshore wind and its attendant sloppy water. To do this, you'll want to point the bow away from shore, allowing you to row clear immediately. You can do this even before you've anchored your feet firmly in the foot stretchers, if you find yourself being blown back onto the beach. A second benefit of pointing the bow away from the beach is that it will give less surface area for an onshore wind and chop to work on. On the negative side, it will mean you'll have to walk farther out into the water to reach the cockpit and board the boat.

Although you may have taken rowing lessons or rowed dealers' boats before you bought your own, your first launching will be both exciting and a little intimidating. There will be no coach or dealer there to watch each move and correct you or make suggestions. Taking a friend along is good for moral support and in case you need a hand. If you can find a friend who has some experience rowing sliding seat, so much the better.

You will probably find it easier to put the oars in the locks, making sure they are on the after side of the pin, and rest the shafts across the boat while she is still on the beach. Be sure the pressure plates of the locks both face the bow: they are designed to take the power of the stroke, while the opposite side of the oarlock is not. If one oarlock is reversed, not only might you damage it, but you will row in wide circles because the arcs of the oars will be different.

Having a friend along will be useful when it comes to getting the boat into the water and getting you into the boat. After the boat is in the water, have your friend either sit on or hold the stern. This will provide the extra stability you need to feel secure in your first boarding. While he balances the boat, you can get aboard, get the sculls sorted out, and get your feet in the stretchers.

As soon as you put your first foot aboard the boat, balance will become more important to you than it has been since the first day you took the training wheels off your two-wheeler. Once you're comfortable, with the oars square to the hull and the blades flat on the water, have your friend release the stern and experiment with the feel of the boat. Sit quietly for a moment just to get the sensation of being aboard, then move your body gently from side to side and feel the oars stabilize you. After you have convinced yourself the boat is stable in that position, move the oars up and down independently of each other and notice the movement of the boat. This little drill will teach you that as long as the oars are square to the hull, blades cupped up with their backs resting on the water, you are very stable. If you begin to feel unstable in the boat, go back to this position and you will instantly stabilize. Whatever you do, don't let go of the oars.

If you need to use both hands for some chore, such as putting on a pair of socks, adjusting the foot stretchers, or lacing up the clogs, the oars can still stabilize you. Simply lean over the crossed shafts and hold them captive between your legs and trunk. In this position, the oars will stabilize the boat, and you will have your hands free.

You shouldn't row away from shore without first thinking of how you are going to get back. When you come in, you'll want to approach the beach at about a 45-degree angle. Once you are about two oar lengths off the sand, kick the stern around so that you are parallel to the beach. To do this, stabilize the boat with the water-side oar, then give one or two short strokes with the land-side oar. Once you are parallel to the beach, stabilize the boat and get out. Even though your recreational boat is toughly constructed and can survive beachings, it's not a good habit to get into; eventually, you would wear away the gelcoat and begin to abrade the fiberglass cloth.

Before you start pulling on the oars, here's something to think about. Most rowing coaches will tell you that the gender of their students makes a major difference in how they learn to row. Before people experience it, they perceive rowing as an "arms" sport. This myth has been around for years, and before the sliding seat, it was true. Today, however, the truth is that rowing is a "leg and back" sport, arms being only the third most important muscle group. Because of this misperception, men, who are used to doing everything with their arms, tend to try to overpower the boat. Most men must learn to think in terms of lifting heavy objects, an activity for which they would use the power of their legs. Men must also think technique—technique for speed, technique before power.

In the beginning, all oarsmen will catch crabs—that is, be unable to get the blade out of the water at the release. If you are rowing with more power than technique, a crab can actually pitch you out of the boat. This is a hard and humbling way to learn that you have fed power into your stroke before you were ready for it. You will also have a myriad of balance problems if you try to row too hard too soon.

Women are used to compensating for their lack of upper body strength by doing things more efficiently with their legs and back, and that's the secret to rowing. Because they are not as strong, women tend to learn technique before men. For both sexes, the key to rowing is technique, which may be harder for men than women. If you are a man, try not to be macho; don't try to row like an Olympian the first day out. Rowing takes practice, but it's worth it.

After you've learned about balance and repeated to yourself a hundred times, "technique, technique," have your friend take hold of or straddle your stern again. Go into the layback position and check your foot stretchers. Do this with the blades in the water, as this will be more stable than if you tried to hold them above the surface. If you find your stretchers are wrong by half an inch or so, don't worry about it. Just remember to correct them when you get out of the boat. If, however, you find that they are off by an inch or two, you will have to get out of the boat and reposition them before rowing. Don't be surprised if they seem different when the boat is afloat than they did when the boat was on the beach—this happens. After the foot stretchers, check the height of your oarlocks by going to the release position with the blades buried; see that your hands come to your body at the abdomen. Once that's completed, it's time to start rowing, always remembering, "technique, not strength, technique, not speed."

You will probably want your friend to keep holding or sitting on the stern during your first couple of strokes. Of course, if you are alone, you can still learn to row—it's just easier with someone there to spot for you. Before your first stroke, you'll want to get the proper grip on the oar handles. You don't have to hold them as if you were trying to choke the life out of them. Think of your hands as hooks, and hook the handles by the fingers; don't grasp the handles in the palms of your hands. Your thumbs should push against the ends of the handles. This accomplishes two things: it keeps your hands from slipping down the handles as you row, and it keeps the cheek of the button in contact with the inboard face of the oarlock. This slight pressure against the tip of the handle is another factor that affects your balance. Having the sculls firmly pressed against the oarlock will make you feel more secure in the boat.

Technique

Starting the stroke from the catch position will be the most comfortable for you because, next to the rest position, it is the most stable. Don't worry about feathering for the first few strokes; simply keep the blade square and go through the sequence. To get into the catch position, lean toward the stern, pivoting at the hips, and extend your arms straight in front of you; then slide toward the stern, bending your knees but maintaining the same body angle. As you do this, run through the sequence in your head; it will give your brain something to work on. The sequence is legs, back, arms. At the recovery, the arms come away, the back comes over, the legs come up; on the pull-through, legs come down, back swings over, and arms come in. With this chant running through your mind, lower the oar blades into the water by rotating your arms at the shoulders. Straighten your legs against the rigid lever of your back. As the legs straighten, the back should open up and finally the arms pull in. Lift the blades, push the arms away from your body, lean forward, then come down the slide to the catch position. You will probably be quite jerky at first and glad you have a friend holding or sitting on your stern.

Repeat the stroke several times, and once you feel comfortable, have your friend release the stern. Before you get too far from shore, you should know how to turn around. If you do need to make a turn, go to the rest position, and leave the oar on the side toward which you intend to turn square to the boat and resting on the surface of the water with the blade cupped up. Then take short strokes with the other oar. Don't worry about using back or legs, just do short arm strokes. Now that you know how to turn the boat, to get back to the beach or avoid an obstacle, practice your stroke; try to maintain a rhythm so you get the feeling of one stroke flowing into the next.

As stated earlier, balance is going to be very important to you on this first outing, and you will find that nearly everything you do affects it. You will need to "keep your head in the boat," meaning you can't be looking around too much. The head should be kept stationary, looking dead aft. If you find the boat is leaning down to port, it is probably because you have too much clearance between your hands at the crossover. This happens because people are worried about hitting the knuckles of their right hand with the left, but the hands should actually touch, both as they come away on the recovery and on the pull-through. They should be on the same horizontal plane as much as possible, and this will stabilize the boat.

Some other factors that will affect your balance are synchronizing the oars as they enter and leave the water and the speed of the slide in your recovery. At the catch, the blades should drop as one; at the release, they should come out together. Throughout the entire stroke, the oars should be thought of as a single entity, not as individual components. When you start feathering, it will be very important that the oars come out square, then feather. A clean release is not only important to balance, but also to your endurance and back, as blades leaving the water out of square tend to try to lift heavy shovelfuls of water.

Controlling the speed of the slide on recovery is also a factor of balance. Some beginners feel out of balance when their oars are out of the water; therefore they rocket down the slide to get their oars back in the water as soon as possible. In fact, this only upsets the boat's balance. To maintain balance, the ratio of time for stroke to time for recovery must be less than 1:1. Each boat is different, but a 1:1½ ratio might be a good place to start, and a 1:2 ratio is not unheard of. You can demonstrate this fact for yourself. Get up some speed, then do a couple of strokes with an exaggeratedly fast recovery and feel the boat. After the boat calms down, do a second pair of strokes with very slow slides and feel the difference.

With all this in mind, go on rowing. Don't try for speed or power, simply practice the sequence of the stroke. Unless you are about to hit something, don't worry about trying to row in a straight line. If you do, you'll be constantly rowing with one oar and then the other, trying to maintain the course you set for yourself instead of learning the sequence. Rowing a good course will come naturally as your skill improves.

If you feel tippy, slow down. If you still feel unstable, go into the rest position for a short time until you feel better. If you feel yourself becoming nervous, stop at the rest position. It is nearly impossible to keep to the sequence while you are nervous, and not keeping to the sequence will make you more nervous. Try not to get frustrated—rowing is fun, rowing is relaxing. There's a first time for everyone.

Once you begin to feel more comfortable in the boat and with your stroke, try feathering, being careful to avoid one practice in particular that could very quickly become a bad habit. As with all bad habits, it is easier not to start than to correct it. This particular bad-habit-to-be is the practice of tapping the blades on the surface of the water during recovery. Many beginners do this because they mistakenly feel it gives them extra balance. In fact, it slows the boat down, and if one oar catches some chop, it could disrupt the balance substantially. Get the oars out of the water at the release and keep them out until the catch. There are no halfway measures here. You can't lift the oars for part of the stroke and let them slide on the surface for the rest of it, and you can't let them tap on the surface at intervals. If the oars touch the water at different times, the one that touched first will suck its side down, destabilizing the boat. This will probably cause you to overcompensate with the other oar and set up a rocking motion from side to side. If you find yourself tapping the water when you start feathering your oars, push your hands down slightly. If this doesn't help, go back to no-feather rowing for ten or twenty strokes, then try again.

Hopefully, your first outing in the new boat will be long enough to give you a good feeling for her. Don't worry about how far you row or where you go, just get comfortable with the boat. If you find your balance isn't what you think it should be, there are a couple of drills you can try that should improve it.

The first is simply no-feather rowing. This will help you clean up your blade work and overcome the desire to tap your oars during the recovery. This drill will be much easier if you have some speed before you start, so get the boat moving, and then switch to no-feather. If the bottom edge of the blade catches on the surface of the water, force it on through. After ten or twenty strokes, go back to feather rowing and see if you can feel the difference.

The second drill is a pause drill, which will help you control the speed of your slide. A pause drill is both simple and effective. A pause drill, as the name implies, simply requires that you pause in the stroke. Once you have released, brought your arms away from the body, and pivoted into the lean-forward position, you pause before taking the slide. Stop in that position for one and a half to two seconds, then make a very slow and deliberate slide. Ten to twenty strokes with the pause drill should be enough to make a difference.

COMMON PROBLEMS

There are some common problems that beginners tend to suffer, some of which, like tapping the water during recovery, can become bad habits. Others can prevent you from becoming efficient in your rowing. Still others could cause pain if they are not corrected.

The first problem many coaches notice is that their students lift with their backs to put the oars in the water at the catch, instead of swiveling their arms at the shoulders. This is called "rowboat" or "dory-style" rowing, rowing in an oval pattern rather than keeping your movement parallel to the water. There are two ways to detect this, either by the feel of your body or by having a friend on the beach watch for it.

A second problem is lack of discipline in the hands, as in not rolling the oars all the way up to the square position before the catch. This causes the oars to enter the water under-squared and to dig deep or "knife in." If this is not corrected, it will encourage dory-style rowing. A more subtle form of dory-style rowing also encouraged by the lack of hand discipline is known as "over-the-hill" rowing, in which the back goes through its proper swing but the arms take on an oval route. Again, the feel of your stroke will indicate if this is a problem; so will your oar blades' depth on the pull-through, which an observer can also spot.

The length of your stroke will be very important to you as you progress in the sport. Here, there are three mistakes beginners tend to make that should be recognized and dealt with as soon as they appear. Many cut their layback short because it feels uncomfortable and unstable. You must go back to about 15 degrees of layback or you will lose all the power at the finish of the pull-through, effectively cutting short the stroke. Conversely, some over-achievers go to extremes. If you end up doing a sit-up on each stroke, you will be working your body too hard and not gaining enough added speed to make the extra strain worth the exertion. As you row, you will begin to feel more comfortable in the proper lean-back position, and your body will tell you when it is exceeding that 15-degree angle. At the other end of the stroke—the catch—some try for too much reach. After you get the proper body angle, leaning forward out of the recovery, maintain it. Don't get to the catch and try to reach out more or lunge into more angle. You don't really gain anything by doing this, and the sudden shift of weight can sink the stern slightly, checking the run of the boat. Be aware of your forward lean from the start of the slide, and keep it the same at the catch.

An uncontrolled slide is another fault coaches regularly observe in their beginning students. Along with feeling insecure in the recovery and hastening the slide to get the oars back in the water, some students see a quick slide as a way to increase speed. The converse is in fact true; a controlled slide increases speed. Slamming back into the foot stretchers, like lunging to gain extra reach at the catch, simply scrubs off speed. The weight of your body rocketing aft sinks, or checks, the stern and virtually stops the boat. Then you have to get it moving again on the next stroke. The boat must be allowed to work for you, to "run." The same 1:1½ or 1:2 ratio of stroke to recovery that helps you maintain your balance will allow the boat to work for you throughout the recovery. The more proficient you become, the more you will be able to feel what is right for your boat.

Putting the oars in the water seems to bother a lot of people new to sculling. Aside from the problems of getting both oars in and out of the water at precisely the same time, there are some other difficulties encountered in this area. One is known as "skying the blades," which consists of lifting the blades just before the catch. This is caused by dipping the hands down just before you roll the blades up into the square position. Most people do this in an attempt to keep the oars from tapping on the water before the catch. As long as you haven't lifted your hands during the recovery, you don't need to take this precaution; the blades will square up and drop directly into the water without tapping. Skying the blades upsets the balance of the boat by disrupting its flow; it's not natural for the oars to go up, then down. They should go straight back, then into the water, with you swiveling at the shoulder joint to place them. Having a friend on the beach can help you. It's hard for the beginning rower to concentrate on everything at once, and skying the blades is a problem that is more noticeable from outside the boat.

Another problem with putting the oars in the water that your friend on the beach can spot is that of splash. The most common problem is excessive back splash—that is, splash toward the bow, off the back of the blade. This is caused by putting the oars in the water too soon, and it cuts the length of the stroke and puts the brakes on the boat. You want to put the blades in the water during the last one to two inches of recovery. The perfect sculler will have no back splash, but in reality, we should think in terms of how little back splash we can create. Very little back splash, say, two to four inches, is acceptable. More than that is not. If your spotter on the beach tells you that a three-foot wave is coming off the blades, delay putting the blades in a little more at each catch, until your friend informs you that the back splash is insignificant.

If there is no back splash, either you are the perfect sculler or there is front splash. While a modicum of back splash is acceptable, no front splash should be allowed. Front splash, water deflected off the face of the blade toward the stern, is caused by putting the blade in the water after you've completed part of the pull-through. The oar is actually hitting the water after your legs have started their drive. This shortens the stroke and robs power from the beginning of the pull-through. If you see this splash out of the corner of your eye or your spotter on the beach calls your attention to it, simply put the blade in the water a little sooner, always keeping in mind the pitfalls of back splash. Be sure the blades are in the water before your legs start their drive.

BACKING AND TURNING

After you've become comfortable rowing back and forth, have found your stroke to be acceptable, and have practiced turning the boat, there is a pair of maneuvers that you should learn. You may not attempt these your first time out, but as soon as you feel ready, you should learn both backing and the spin turn. Either can get you out of trouble, and they are handy skills to have in your repertoire.

Backing, as the name implies, refers to rowing the boat backwards. To accomplish this, start in at the forward end of the slide with the rest position, then roll the oars so the blades face the bow. Without using the slide, draw the oar handles to your abdomen, lower the blades into the water, and push away with your arms. Don't try to feather or take overly long strokes; square blades and short strokes are the trick to this maneuver. You may feel out of balance at first, but as with everything else, it will come.

The spin turn is a faster way to get the boat to turn through 45 to 360 degrees—faster than rowing with a single oar. There are actually two ways to accomplish a spin turn. Which one you choose to use will depend to a great extent upon the stability of your boat and how comfortable you feel aboard her. The first and most stable method of making a spin turn requires that you go to the rest position in the middle of the slide. While the blade of one oar rests with its scoop up on the surface of the water, roll the other oar so that the scoop of the blade faces the stern. Push the handle away from you, place the blade in the water, and, using only your arm, draw the handle to your abdomen. Return the oar to the stable rest position, roll the other oar so that the scoop faces the bow, and make a stroke as if you were backing the boat. Repeat this alternating stroke until the boat is facing the proper direction. You will find this much faster than rowing with a single oar. The second method is slightly faster but considerably less stable. You will want to try it only if you feel very secure in the boat. Everything is done as in the first example, except that you move the oars simultaneously; there is no oar in the rest position for balance

After you've spent some time in the boat—enough to be comfortable but not enough to develop bad habits—it's time to work on refining your stroke. The perfect rowing stroke—the fastest, most efficient way to move your boat through water—is the subject of Chapter 3.

The Perfect Rowing Stroke

No one has the perfect rowing stroke. Olympic gold medalists don't have it, nor do oarsmen who have been practicing their sport for 45 years. Nevertheless, every sculler strives for it. Why? you might ask. After all, you've finally gotten comfortable in the boat, you don't feel that you're going to fall out on every other stroke, and you can get from point A to point B without too much trouble. Sure, you'll probably admit, the perfect stroke could make you faster, but you're not going to be a national champion, let alone an Olympic sculler, so why strive for the unattainable? What's wrong with continuing the way you've been going?

First of all, it's human nature to want constant improvement. Proficiency at a chosen endeavor is gratifying. You will enjoy your rowing more if you know that you're rowing better in August than you were in June and that you will be still better in September. There is also a theory that speed across the water is directly related to fun on the water. The faster you go, the more fun you have, and you gain speed as you get closer to the perfect stroke.

Human nature and the joy of increased speed aside, there are practical reasons to aspire to the perfect stroke, one of these being the avoidance of pain. You can hurt yourself by rowing improperly. In fact, you can develop major lower-back pain from either "dory-style" rowing or from using your back too soon on the drive. Even if you don't sustain injury, you will find that a less-than-proper stroke is not as efficient, and this means that a workout will be harder on your body if you lack proper technique.

To improve your stroke, you must first have the right mental set. There is a common fallacy, especially among beginners, that the stroke has a "beginning" and a "finish." In fact, the stroke is a continuous, fluid motion that merges into the next stroke, and the one after that. You "begin" when you first strike the water at your first catch of the day, and you "finish" when you release for the last time; between those two moments, everything should flow together.

THE PERFECT STROKE

With the concept of "flow" firmly in mind, we will go through the sequence of a single stroke. The catch is the normal place to begin for two reasons. It is a stable position, and it is the beginning of the power portion of the stroke. At the catch, you are leaning forward over your knees with your ankles just a couple of degrees shy of the vertical and your oars squared up and just off the water. To take the water, or initiate the catch, pivot from your shoulder sockets, lifting the hands a couple of inches, with the arms straight. There is no lifting of the back at this point; you don't use your back to put the oars in the water. It's all a motion of the hands and arms. You want to consciously flex your lats (the latissimus dorsi); if they are not flexed, your back will stretch, robbing power from the drive of your legs. Your arms are also set; they may want to take the catch, but they're not strong enough. That is why the legs supply the power. As the oars enter the water, your legs start to push. At this point, nothing else is happening. The oars have entered the water, and the legs have begun their drive. The back is set against the legs, maintaining the same forward angle. The power of the legs is transferred through the rigid back and arms to the oars.

When the legs are about halfway down, the back begins to open up. As it swings, your shoulders, like your hands, move on a horizontal plane; they do not lift vertically. At the same time, the arms begin to bend. Use your lats, not your biceps, to bend the arms. This gives an entirely different feel, the elbows coming in near the sides of the

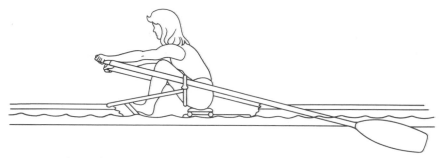

At the catch, the arms are straight and locked, the body bent forward, the knees compressed, and the heels raised.

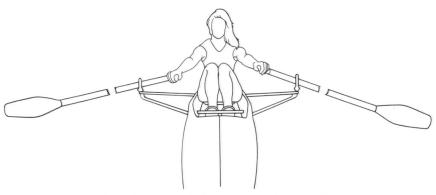

The catch as seen from the stern. The knees are together, and the thumbs are on the ends of the oar handles, where they supply a light pressure to keep the buttons in contact with the locks.

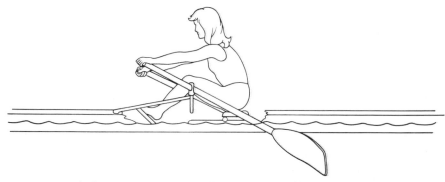

At the beginning of the drive, the legs supply all the power. The arms are still straight, acting as levers to deliver the power to the oars, and the back is still bent.

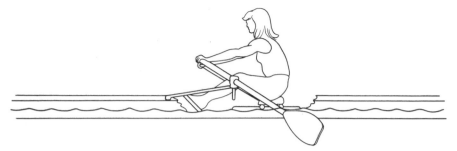

As the legs come down, the back just begins to open up. The arms remain locked.

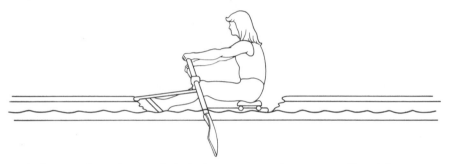

The legs are almost down, and the back is swinging. The arms are still straight.

body, then sweeping past. If you were to use your biceps, the arms would "chicken-wing," raising the elbows upward. At the moment the legs flatten out, the back should reach its layback position, and the arms will finish their pull. All through the drive, the oars should move on a horizontal plane through the water, not in an oval. The blades should be just covered; in fact, if you glance at them out of the corner of your eye, you should be able to see what appears to be a mound of water traveling with them. If you don't see this moving mound, or "bubble," your blades are too deep. Rowing with your blades deep affects your balance, and it is inefficient because it also decreases leverage.

Your hands should finish the drive somewhere between your bellybutton and sternum. If they come into your lap, you will lift your oars too early and cut the length of your stroke. When the hands come into your body, push them straight down into your lap, making a square corner as you lift the blades. The blades should still be squared up as they leave the water. If you feather a fraction of a

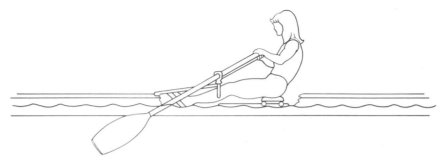

The arms pull last, finishing at the sternum as the body achieves its full backward lean.

The hands drop straight to the lap, lifting the blades before they are feathered.

second too early, the blades will meet a lot of resistance as they emerge, and you may catch a crab. When the lower edges of the blades are free, feather by rolling up your hands.

As soon as the blades are feathered, push your arms away from your body, getting their weight out of the bow quickly. When the arms are nearly straight, your body swings forward, pivoting at the hips. Not only does the weight of your head and trunk then come out of the bow, but at this point you're setting the angle of forward lean to use at the next catch. As we saw in Chapter 2, if you try to get more forward lean just before the catch, you will check the stern of the boat, cutting short its run. Therefore, only when your hands are over your knees and you've achieved all your forward lean do your legs begin to bend. You can't let your muscles lose control on the slide, or you'll rush, checking the boat. Your hamstrings must control the slide, giving you the proper ratio of recovery to drive, as discussed in Chapter 2. As your legs begin to bend and your entire body starts out of the bow, you begin to rotate your wrists to square up the blades for the strike of the next catch. The blades must be squared before you pivot your arms to take the water. Otherwise, you may have to break the flow of the

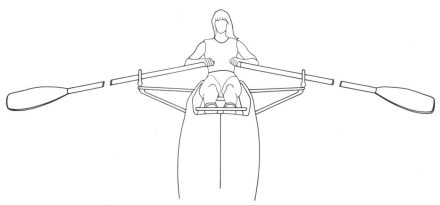

The release as seen from the stern. The hands have just finished at the base of the sternum and are dropping into the lap, releasing the blades. The elbows are kept low.

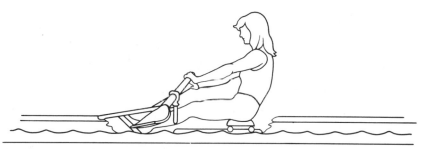

On the recovery, the arms are extended first. Then the body leans forward, and finally, the legs control the recovery down the slide.

stroke to square up, or risk having the blades strike obliquely and "knife in."

The perfect stroke doesn't take long to read about, but you can spend a lifetime attempting to master it. There are hundreds of points to remember about each stroke, and since all the movements are interconnected, each has an effect on the one after it and the one after that. If you become too compressed at the catch, if your ankles go past 90 degrees, there will be no power in the beginning of your drive. If your oars dig too deep in the drive, not only are they inefficient, but they make the release more difficult. If you hurry your recovery, you will both unbalance the boat and check the stern, so that you need to get her started again on the next stroke. Everything is connected, everything flows, from strike to release and from stroke to stroke. You must remember to think of it that way—a continuous, flowing motion.

This motion is the result of every muscle group in your body working in concert. Knowing which muscles are supposed to be working at which times will let you feel when the stroke is correct. The more you get used to this feeling, the sooner you'll notice the strange sensation that signals something amiss. Therefore, it's important to understand the muscles that control your rowing—what they do, and when they make their contribution.

As you strike, the anterior deltoids place the oars, and a fraction of a second later the lats, biceps, triceps, flexors, and all the little muscles in your hands flex to transfer the power from the legs through the back and arms to the oars. As the legs come down, the triceps engage to help the lats as the boat picks up speed, and the gastrocnemii in the calves also come into play. In the layback, the abdominals and the radialis are working, and the pectorals and biceps push the oars away from the body while the abdominals remain flexed. Then the body swings forward, with the lumbar triangle supplying the motive force. As the body starts the recovery, the hamstrings control the very important speed of the slide.

When you have rowed long enough that the newness of the sport has worn off and you've become accustomed to how you feel after an outing, listening to your body can tell you a lot. For example, if your abdominals are considerably more sore than usual, you may be getting excessive layback at the release, and your stomach muscles are having to pull you up as they would for a sit-up. If the flexors of your forearms are tight and sore, you were probably holding the oars too tightly. Your body should feel the same after each workout. If it doesn't, try to figure out why. Listening to your body is one way to monitor your performance.

FINE-TUNING YOUR BOAT

As you become more proficient in your stroke, you may need to fine-tune the boat. Your body will change as you row, and you will have to make alterations to the rig to match. At the same time, you will become more familiar with the boat, and your stroke will improve. Some of the early adjustments you made to compensate for your lack of experience will have to be altered.

If you have lost a significant amount of weight, you will notice that the clearance on each recovery is excessive. To bring the boat back in line with your body, you will want to decrease the height of the riggers. At the same time, you might look at the difference in height between the port and the starboard rigger. That difference must be sufficient to allow for proper left-over-right rowing, but you may have become familiar enough with the technique to tolerate an eighth of an inch less and still keep your hands clear. Anything you can take out is good, because it will bring the oars closer to the same horizontal plane.

While working on the locks, you will want to decrease their pitch. You should have set it unnaturally high—6 degrees of positive pitch—when you first started rowing, because it helped you at the release. Now that you are more competent you will want to take the pitch down, making it easier to keep the oars in the water. Don't take them immediately down to 3 degrees, but if you take one or two degrees out, you will feel the difference. Again, if you reduce the pitch too much, you will develop a tendency to "knife in" and dig too deep.

After you adjust the rig, you may want to experiment with where you sit. As scullers become comfortable in their boats they often want to sit a little farther away from their oars, and they move the stretchers toward the bow. You lengthen your stroke by not sitting hunched over the oars and by allowing your body to swing. This is the time to really work at getting your stretchers properly set. Until this time, if they were within an inch of being correct you could live with it, but now that you're trying to refine your stroke, they should be set properly.

Stretcher tuning is limited to coarse adjustments in most recreational boats. In many, the stretchers are adjusted by one-inch increments. In some, tuning is limited to two-inch adjustments. If your stretchers can't be moved to the desired position, don't be afraid to make some minor modifications to the system. You can either drill new mounting holes or use shims to position your feet properly. Don't accept what you've been given if it's wrong; you'll pay for it in the end.

REFINING YOUR TECHNIQUE

After you've retuned your boat to match the changes in your body and ability, you will have to concentrate on yourself. All the problems you had to deal with when you first began to row sliding-seat (which were discussed at length in Chapter 2) can rear their heads again and again, each time more insidiously than the last. Your hands can begin "over-the-hill" rowing so gradually that you won't notice it until it becomes a major problem. Your blades may tap the surface on every third or fourth recovery, then every other stroke, and so on, until you're sliding them along the surface of the water on each recovery, scrubbing speed off the run. Your blades can dig deeper and deeper with each mile you row, becoming ever less efficient. Skying the blades can start by dipping your hands just a quarter of an inch, and it may go from there until finally, you'll be terribly out of balance just before each catch and will have no idea how you got that way. Then there is the speed of the slide, which can creep up until your ratio is 1:1, unbalancing the boat and wearing you out. If you stay constantly aware of each and every movement, you can halt these creeping inefficiencies before they become bad habits.

As your stroke improves, other problems become important to deal with. If you were "bucking the oars" or "bucketing" when you first started rowing, it wasn't all that important. The important thing was to get used to the rhythm of the stroke and the balance of the boat. Now that you are concentrating on the length and flow of your stroke, however, you can't permit either of these style faults. "Bucking the oars" refers to shortening the finish before the hands have come all the way to the body. To get the proper length at this end of your stroke, you must go all the way into your layback and bring the oars right up to your body. "Bucketing" also happens at the forward end of the stroke, but takes place during the recovery. "Bucketing" consists of lunging forward with the body before the arms have straightened out. This disrupts both the slide and the balance of the boat.

There is no way to rationalize any of these style faults. Coaches have heard every possible excuse. They don't believe them, and you shouldn't either when you try to justify to yourself a compromise in your style.

One of the most common problems scullers have when they begin to improve is understanding that the number of strokes per minute cannot be equated with power and speed through the water. They begin to rationalize speeding their slide as a way to take up the stroke rate. In fact, you can row 10 strokes per minute at full power with a high ratio of recovery to stroke, or 40 strokes per minute with almost no power and a very low ratio. One will be efficient and will save your body; the other will be inefficient and will sap your stamina. East

German Olympic and world-class rowers train for hours at full power while rowing 18 strokes per minute. Gordie Nash trained for and won the 1984 Catalina–Marina del Rey Race, a 35-mile open-ocean endurance test, rowing 22 strokes per minute. A powerful stroke combined with a low stroke rate is more efficient, both for moving the boat through the water and for conserving strength. You can go much farther this way and still have something left for the finish.

If, during a race, you are nearing the finish line bow to bow with your archrival, or if you're in the middle of a channel trapped between an oncoming ferry and a commercial fishing boat, you can gain needed speed by taking the stroke rate up, but you have to do it properly. Simply flailing away with the oars and rocketing up and down the slide won't make you go any faster. In fact, it may slow you down.

If you want to take the stroke up, it must be done first with the hands, then the body, and last, the legs. At the release, you will push your arms away from your body faster, and swing the body into the forward lean position more quickly (being careful not to "bucket"), *but*, as soon as you have your full forward lean, *control the slide.* If you don't, you will check the stern and more than counteract any gains you were making by taking up the rate. As you do take up your rate, you will find that the speed of your drive increases slightly. Therefore, the speed of your recovery can increase correspondingly, but it must always be controlled, and the proper ratio must be kept in mind.

If you want to prove to yourself just how important a controlled slide is to speed, endurance, and balance, find a pair of buoys or landmarks about a quarter of a mile apart. First row the distance with your body flying up and down the slide, with a stroke rate between 35 and 40 per minute. When you finish, make a mental note of how you feel and how the boat felt. After you've taken a breather, row back the other way, concentrating on power in the pull-through and a very slow slide. Keep your rate between 20 and 22 strokes per minute. After your second pass over the measured distance, compare how you feel and how the boat felt to the first pass.

There are some drills you can do each time you start a row that will set you up, physically and mentally, for the proper stroke. When you first row away from the dock or beach, try about 50 strokes of no-leg rowing. To do this, set your legs straight, but don't lock the knees; they should have a little flex. Then start rowing without using the legs, simply swinging the body fore and aft. This will warm up the back and abdomen and stretch the hamstrings. After 50 strokes, feed in about

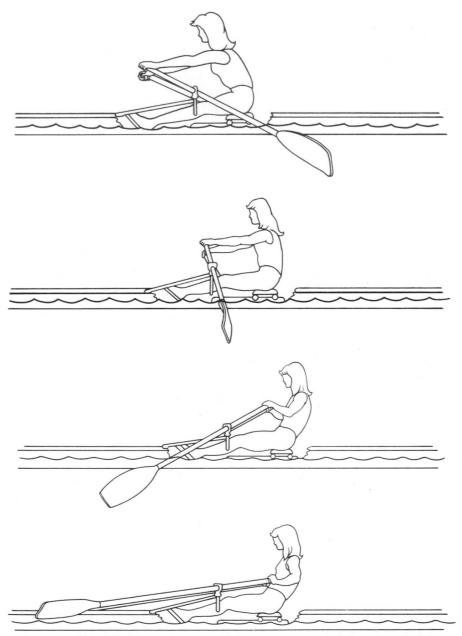

No-leg rowing. Your body swings and your arms move normally, but your legs remain stationary.

half the slide, still swinging the body. This will work the legs into the stroke gradually. After 50 repetitions of the half slide, you will be ready to go to full slide.

If your oars are tapping the water on recovery, or if your release hasn't been as clean as it should be, you might want to initiate a no-feather rowing drill as soon as you've warmed up your legs and lengthened to a full stroke. Done as a drill, no-feather rowing is a little more involved than was discussed in Chapter 2. You'll need to start with some speed for stability, then square up the blades and set the wrists. Be prepared to carry your hands slightly lower through the recovery than you would when feathering, and be ready to feel the boat lurch. If the lower edge of a blade catches the water, the boat will lurch toward the side that hit. Don't stop, and don't cheat and feather at this point; push the blade on through. If the boat stops, revert to feathered rowing to regain speed and balance, then force yourself to go back to no-feather. You must complete at least 10 strokes in this no-feather drill to make it worthwhile. In the beginning, it will be terribly frustrating, but it can be done, and the results will justify your efforts.

Those three drills—no-leg rowing, half-slide rowing, and no-feather rowing—will start your row in the proper way. You will be loose, warmed up, and ready for a good row. There is also a cool-down drill to follow. It's alright to come to the beach sweaty, but you shouldn't come in breathing hard, with your heart pounding. About a half- to a quarter-mile from the beach or dock, paddle down for a few strokes, then initiate a pause drill. The pause drill, discussed in Chapter 2, will help you control the speed of your slide and will cool you down.

MARKING YOUR PROGRESS

There are two ways to monitor the improvement of your stroke. The first consists of simply watching your "puddles," the boils left in the water by your release. The spacing between these disturbances will give you a very accurate indication of how efficient your stroke is. Of course, if your stroke rate is not constant, the distance between the puddles will vary; if your rate is consistent, however, the spacing will be an invaluable, easy-to-use tool. The greater the distance between puddles, the more efficient your stroke. Obviously, the distance between the puddles will differ from boat to boat and vary with

weather conditions. You cannot expect a 16-foot, 65-pound Alden
Single to carry way exactly as a 26-foot, 28-pound racing shell does,
and your run won't be as long in a head wind and chop as in glass-
smooth water. Nevertheless, once you've observed your spacing in a
variety of conditions, you will have a good idea of where the puddles
should be. If you are used to seeing your puddles three feet off the
stern as you strike the water at your next catch, and suddenly they are
flanking your stern as you strike, you'll know you are rushing the
recovery.

A second way to monitor your efficiency is by taking your heart rate.
You may, for example, row a distance of two miles in 20 minutes,
finding that your heart rate at the end is 150. This becomes your base
rate. Turn your attention to a particular problem that you need to work
on, such as tapping your blades during recovery or sloppy blade work
at the release, and concentrate on it until you have it under control,
whether it takes a week or a month. Then do your base distance again
under similar conditions. If you cover your two miles in less than 20
minutes and your heart is still at 150 when you finish, you have
become more efficient.

HANDLING ROUGH WEATHER

As you improve your stroke, become more comfortable in the boat,
and get into better shape, you will start rowing farther. This may
expose you to more open water and different conditions. When you
find yourself in rough water, you'll probably experience two
problems: lack of stability and difficulty in getting the oars across the
water during the recovery. To improve your stability, you will have to
shorten the stroke. This doesn't mean using less of the slide; it means
cutting both the forward lean at the catch and the layback at the
release. These are the two least stable positions when rowing, and
eliminating or at least reducing the angle of each will go a long way
toward making the boat more stable. If the water is really rough, the
oar blades are going to slam into the chop no matter how far down you
push your hands during recovery. Try reducing the amount of
feathering. If you don't feather all the way—that is, if you roll the
handles through 45 degrees instead of 90, the blades will strike the
chop at an angle. The boat will still rock, but when the rounded back

of the blade is presented to the chop at an angle, the blade will tend to lift, minimizing the effect of the impact.

When you encounter a head wind, you will want to delay your roll-up (the squaring of the blades before they strike water). The longer you delay it, the less time the blade will be square to the wind and chop. You will feel the wind on the blades, but the real benefit of delaying your roll-up until the last possible moment is that the chop won't strike the squared-up blade. A steep chop could actually knock the blade out of your hand, and just the possibility of this happening will probably make you tighten your grip on the handle, resulting in forearm cramps. The delayed roll-up should not become a habit that you carry over to flat water. If you do, it will encourage you either to pause before you strike, breaking the rhythm of your stroke, or strike under-squared, which will drag the oar deep.

In a downwind situation, you will probably find you're having a little problem balancing the boat. On the other hand, you'll have added speed. You can shorten your stroke the same way you would in a head wind to stabilize the boat, but you'll want to stay as long as possible to take advantage of the extra speed. The extra speed of downwind rowing can be exhilarating, but it can also be dangerous, especially in open water.

If it's quite rough and you find yourself surfing the wind waves, you will want to shorten your stroke, especially at the release. By reducing your layback, you will keep weight out of the bow. If your weight is too far forward when you come off the face of a wave, you can bury your bow, causing the boat to spin out. As the unweighted stern spins around, it may force the oar on the side toward which it is spinning to bury, either pulling the oar out of your hand or actually disrupting your balance enough to pitch you out of the boat. If you begin to take off on a wave that you think is too big, slide your weight right aft to keep the bow up. If you start to broach, you can drag the tip of a blade, turning the boat toward that side and straightening it out again. After your initial experience, you may find windy days quite exciting, and look forward to riding the chop.

In smooth water, be aware of your stroke, making it long, fluid, and well timed. As your stroke improves and becomes steadier, you will need to develop your steering skills; you will not want to stop, row with one oar in order to correct course, then pick up the stroke again. Before you can steer, you must first set your course. Pick a destination, making sure the course is clear of buoys or any other obstruction, then point your bow toward it. With your boat lined up, find a spot directly astern as a reference point. If you begin to drift off, realign yourself by reaching out a little farther with one oar at the catch, and the extra power will turn you. Reference to a stern point doesn't mean you should never look over your shoulder. There might be something in the water you missed when you set your course, and there may be other boats, swimmers, or windsurfers sharing the water with you, so glance forward every ten strokes or so. The best time to look over your shoulder is in the middle of your pull-through, when the oars are in the water providing stability.

Rowing is a constant learning experience. Each time you practice the sport, you will learn something new or refine a previously acquired skill, but the practice can be an end in itself. The exercise of rowing feels good and is good. Monitoring your stroke and seeing the improvements in efficiency over the long run provides one of the many rewards of rowing.

Oars, Accessories, and Maintenance

An aesthetically pleasing boat is more fun to row, so to a large extent, the overall appearance of your recreational rowing boat and its equipment will determine your enjoyment of each outing aboard her. Keeping your boat in top shape will also help retain the value of your investment. Maintaining a fair bottom will allow the boat to work at its best, giving you the most out of each stroke. A clean, well-maintained boat simply performs better and encourages you to do the same.

Your recreational boat is, in fact, a highly tuned assembly of components. Each element must be chosen for compatibility with the others, and must be maintained properly to operate efficiently. The number of component parts is small and their maintenance is a simple matter, but it must be done, or your rowing program will suffer.

The components of your boat can be divided into six groups: the sculls, riggers and oarlocks, seat and tracks, foot stretchers, accessories you've added to the boat, and, of course, the hull. Except for any modifications you've made, all these items should come with the boat when you buy it. Depending upon where you buy it and what kind of package deal is offered, you may have quite a bit of latitude in selecting your own gear, so we'll look at the differences in equipment along with the way you'll need to care for it.

THE SCULLS

There are two basic scull constructions: wood and carbon fiber. Each has its advantages and disadvantages. Proponents of wooden sculls claim they bite the water better and are quieter in the oarlocks and better looking. Supporters of carbon fiber point out that their sculls are lighter, stiffer, and easier to maintain. Neither faction is wrong. It is simply a matter of what is most important to you.

Wooden sculls, the traditional choice, are usually built of basswood or spruce and are hollow for lightness. They must be handled with a certain amount of care to prevent chipping or splintering. For transporting and storing, the blade covers mentioned in Chapter 2 provide excellent protection for the most vulnerable portion of the sculls, but the shafts also require care in handling. Knocking the shafts on the roof rack of your car, for instance, can ding the protective varnish coat and allow water to seep into the wood. Treat the blades carefully while you are launching, and in shallow water, keep your strokes well clear of the bottom. Buoys and other floating obstacles should be given a wide berth. Remember, with both sculls in the water your beam is nearly 20 feet. Your wooden sculls are going to need to be sanded down and revarnished at regular intervals. How frequently you do this will depend on how much and how carefully you use them.

Wooden sculls do indeed require more maintenance than their carbon fiber counterparts, but many people prefer them. Not only are they more aesthetically pleasing, many claim they are more efficient. The scoops of their blades are far better designed than those of the plastic sculls; while the blades of carbon fiber oars are flat from the top to the bottom edge, wooden blades have deeper, more complex curves, allowing them to hold the water better. For purists, they have other advantages. They are quieter as they rotate in the oarlocks, and many claim that they "feel" better.

Carbon fiber sculls are somewhat tougher, but they should be treated with respect, and blade covers would not be out of place on plastic blades. They are definitely lighter, though it is impossible to say precisely how much. One cannot claim, for example, that carbon fiber sculls are "one-third" or "one-quarter" lighter than wood, simply because wooden sculls vary so much in weight depending on their construction and manufacturer. This difference in weight may not matter over a 2,000-meter course, but if you plan to row long distances, it could be significant. Carbon fiber oars are also stiffer. If you watch a rower switch from wood to carbon, you can see the difference very easily. The wooden oar has much more "whip" than the carbon fiber, and a stiffer oar is a more efficient oar. This stiffness transfers power better, and you can feel it at the catch. Your boat will jump a little more as you put in the power.

The choice between wood and carbon fiber is yours, but don't agonize over it. If you haven't rowed sliding seat before, or if you haven't rowed much, just be sure you get a pair of oars that are well built and matched in weight. Later you may want to switch, but in the beginning there are more important things to concentrate on than the materials from which your sculls are made.

While the material you select for your oars is not a crucial decision, the commitment to maintaining them is. If you choose wood, be prepared to keep the varnish in good condition. It will add years to the life of the sculls. Another maintenance area—that is, the sleeves and buttons—is common to both wood and carbon fiber sculls. In Chapter 2, lubricating the sleeves was mentioned. That advice can only be repeated here. Do not use heavy lubricants such as Crisco or Vaseline. The plastic sleeves on modern sculls need only the lightest application of either a silicone or Teflon spray. Anything heavier will be superfluous and messy at best, and will attract and hold damaging dirt and grit at worst. Grit is the archenemy of your sleeves, buttons, and oarlocks. Any sand or dirt trapped between the rotating oar and the stationary oarlock will eat away at both components and eventually destroy them.

For this reason, never lay your oars flat on any surface. Always prop them up or lay them across end supports (like your gunwales) so sand and dirt won't get on the buttons or sleeves. If you row in salt water, you will want to rinse the sculls with fresh water after each use.

OARLOCKS

The Latanzo oarlock has become the standard of the recreational rowing boat industry. These locks are efficient, inexpensive, and nearly maintenance-free. They need to be kept clean and free of dirt, grit, and any lubrication build-up, but apart from that, you have only to take them off their pins every six months or so and clean both the locks on the pin and the bearing surface of the oarlock. When you

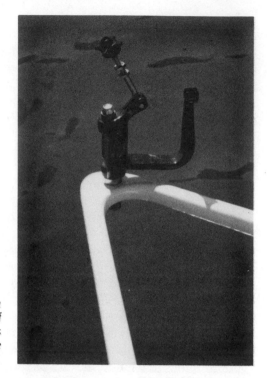

The Latanzo oarlock, shown on the exceptionally clean rigger of an Aero. The twin spacer nuts and the knurled locknut are visible.

remount the locks on the pins, make sure the pitch hasn't changed since the last time you serviced them.

The brass locks that are included with the Oarmaster require even less maintenance than the Latanzos. They must be kept clean to protect the buttons and sleeves, but other than that, they are just about bulletproof.

There are a variety of high-tech oarlocks on the market today, some of which allow you to change pitch simply by inserting a molded shim. These are sleek and very efficient, but be sure they are adaptable to your riggers before you go out and buy them. A hundred dollars is a lot of money to spend on a pair of oarlocks that won't fit your boat.

RIGGERS

Most recreational boats' riggers are stainless steel; some are fiberglass; and others are anodized aluminum. All require very little

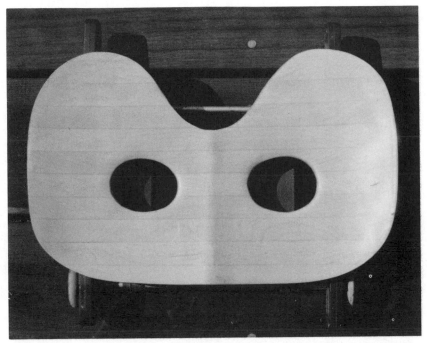

The Latanzo seat. It should be installed so the cutout faces the bow; it is designed to relieve tension on the tailbone.

maintenance. Even stainless steel will develop a thin surface film of rust if it is not kept clean, so give your riggers a quick wipe-down every so often, and they will stay bright for the life of the boat. The aluminum and glass riggers require the same attention. The bolts attaching the riggers to the hull need to be removed about once a year and packed with white grease. This will ensure that you can easily remove them if you ever really need to. The height of Oarmaster riggers is adjusted by a pair of stainless steel bolts in the base of the rigger. When tightened, they act as stops, setting the height of the oarlock. These bolts should be removed and greased more often than once a year, or they will freeze in place with corrosion.

SEAT AND TRACK

Like the Latanzo oarlock, the Latanzo seat and track assembly has also become an industry standard. The anodized aluminum tracks

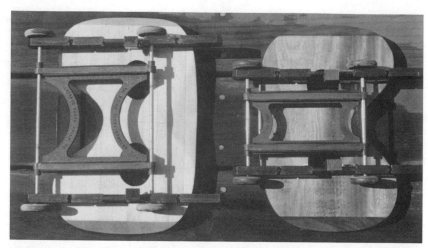

Seats come with different axle lengths, so when ordering a new one, be sure you know this vital measurement.

need to be kept cleared of sand or grit, which will wear down the plastic wheels, and they should be wiped clean every so often. The wheels should not be lubricated; they roll very well without lubrication, and a lubricant becomes gummy with anodization, dirt, and grit, and actually slows the wheels. The seat has a double-action feature: It rolls on the wheels for the length of the track, then slides on the axles to allow a bit more fore-and-aft travel. The axles slide on narrow ribs of the seat's undercarriage. Sometimes these ribs need a tiny amount of the same light lubricant used on the oar sleeves. If you store the boat outside, don't leave the seat in it, because the varnish tends to deteriorate when exposed to sunlight and the elements. If you decide to change to a different seat, be sure the wheels and axle lengths are compatible with your tracks. There are several wheel configurations and at least three standard axle lengths.

The Oarmaster seat is a little different. Instead of having wheels riding inside a cupped track, the Oarmaster unit has cupped wheels that roll on a narrow track, in a configuration reminiscent of train wheels and tracks. The Oarmaster tracks must be kept clean. Some rowers use a very small amount of light lubricant, but this can be messy, and many forgo lubrication without apparent harm. The seat does not have a double action, so there are no axle supports at the ends of the tracks requiring lubrication. Like the Latanzo seat, the

An old-style sliding seat that does not have double action. This type of seat needs longer tracks to get the same layback and compression.

wooden Oarmaster seat should not be exposed to direct sunlight and the elements when the boat is not in use.

Small Craft, Inc., offers the Super Seat, a molded plastic seat that rides on skateboard wheels, which in turn roll on the area of the cockpit where tracks would normally be mounted. Occasionally, perhaps biannually, the wheels should be removed to receive a Teflon spray coat between their bearings and axles. Other than that, the seat seems impervious to hard use. Make sure there is no sand beneath the wide wheels, because the constant rolling of the seat can work the sand like a grinder, cutting away the gelcoat and eventually the glass under it.

FOOT STRETCHERS

Foot stretchers tend to vary more from boat to boat than any other part of the equipment. Keep them clean and rinse them frequently with fresh water. Even if you are the only one using the boat, it is a good idea to check their adjustability on a regular basis and keep them properly lubricated. This will prevent their freezing up and locking in position.

There are a few specific tips for the most common types of stretchers on recreational boats. If your boat came with leather clogs, they will need special care. In addition to rinsing them with fresh, clean water, you will need to treat them occasionally with either saddle soap or Armorall to keep them soft. If track shoes were supplied with your boat, they will need to be cared for as if you were using them as running shoes. Velcro straps, which are common on many boats, can become quite stiff and abrasive as they become salt-encrusted. They should be removed regularly from the boat and soaked in fresh water to rinse out the salt. The metal or plastic cups that support the heels while the feet are held by the Velcro straps usually have drain holes to allow sand and water to wash out. Many rowers find these holes to be inadequate, and drill them out for better drainage.

Sometimes the only wood on a recreational boat is located at the stretchers. If this wood is teak or shedua, it will probably be oiled when the boat arrives. Re-oiling the wood will take almost no time and will keep it bright and protect it as well. If the wood is mahogany or spruce, it was probably varnished at the factory. This means that once a year or so you will need to sand it lightly and put on a fresh coat of good marine varnish. Even if there is no other wood on the boat, the soles of your leather clogs are often wood, and these need the same care as any other wood.

ACCESSORIES

Everything we've discussed to this point either has come with the boat or is absolutely necessary to rowing. There's another group of components, one that varies greatly: custom additions. Before adding anything to your boat, consider it very carefully. Think about the maintenance it may need or the special handling it will require. Also keep in mind that the cockpit of a recreational shell is a limited space, and you won't want to add anything that will take up too much space and inhibit your movement as you slide through the rowing stroke. If you cut a hole through the bottom of the cockpit and install a suction-style bailer, it will require extra care in beach launching and landing. You will have to be careful of sand, which will grind away the bailer's seal. You will also have to be prepared to service and change the seal on a regular basis. If you want to go high-tech and install a digital stroke meter or other electronics, consider that electronic devices and water are natural adversaries, and any electronic aid will require a regular program of preventive maintenance. Before you add something even as commonplace as a water bottle and holder, you will have to consider all your rowing movements so that you don't mount it in the way of your arms, legs, or body. This is not meant to dissuade you from adding anything that you think can improve your performance; it is intended merely to remind you of possible problems.

The list of components you can add to your boat is almost endless. Anything you add, however, will be one more item to lug around and maintain. Each item should pay for the added weight and increased maintenance requirements with greater efficiency, yours or the boat's. Think about each addition before you drill holes and bolt it down. Are you sure you really need it?

THE HULL

Finally, there is the hull itself, which will be either fiberglass or of cold-molded, WEST System construction. For all intents and purposes, a WEST System hull requires the same kind of day-to-day care as "maintenance-free" fiberglass. Anyone who has ever owned a fiberglass boat knows it is not truly maintenance-free, and recreational rowing boats are no different.

If you row in salt water, you will need to rinse the boat with fresh water after each use. Allowed to dry on the boat, salt forms a crusty film that attracts dirt and grime. This accelerates the deterioration of the gelcoat or, in the case of a WEST System boat, the varnish.

All things being equal, the boat should be stored inside, out of the sun and protected from the elements. If this is not possible, it should at least be covered to minimize the effects of sun and rain or snow. Depending upon how often you use the boat and how it's stored, you will want to clean the hull, deck, and cockpit interior regularly with a non-abrasive powder, liquid cleanser, or special fiberglass cleaner. Once a surface is clean, a good buffing will bring back the luster it had when it was new.

Since the bottom of the boat must slide through oil slicks on the water and is dragged across beaches and docks, it requires something extra in the way of maintenance. Any dings must be repaired soon after they appear. If a ding is left unrepaired, it will enlarge and suck up water, making the boat weaker and heavier. Once a ding is repaired with either fiberglass cloth and resin, chopped glass or foam and resin, or resin alone, depending upon the severity of the break, it should be sanded down to restore the fairness of the hull. Even if you have a professional make the repair (which is recommended unless you are an expert with cloth and resin), you should do the sanding yourself, because only an owner will put in the time necessary to achieve perfect fairness. The sanding should be done in the same way a sailor would prepare the bottom of his racing yacht. You will need either a sanding block or a fairing strip, the latter being either a thin piece of wood or a chunk of foam flexible enough to conform to the hull configuration but firm enough to keep the sandpaper in constant contact with the boat. Start with sandpaper in the 220-grit range, and work your way down to the wet-and-dry 600 to finish the job.

Proper care and storage of your boat will slow the process, but eventually any gelcoat finish will start to fade. You can have the boat refinished with polyurethane paints, which will make her look like new, but these paints should be applied by a professional. If you have a WEST System boat, the resins used in its construction are vulnerable to the ultraviolet rays of the sun. For this reason, it is important to keep a good coat of UV-inhibiting varnish on your boat at all times. If you store your boat inside, or if it is well covered, you will probably have to varnish only once a year, after a light sanding. If she is left out in the direct sun and elements, more frequent refinishing will be necessary. Varnish a newly repaired area of the hull as soon as possible.

One final note on caring for your hull. If the boat is stored in a garage, boat house, or other place where it is protected from rain or snow, be sure to open the inspection ports. This will allow air to circulate through the hull and dry out condensation or any small leaks. If the boat is stored outside where this is not possible, at least protect it from moisture, and open the drainage plug with which most boats are equipped. This will dry the interior somewhat, but it will also break the seal of the hull, allowing for air movement. If you don't do this, some real problems are conceivable. Left in the sun, the air inside your boat will expand, and if it is trapped, it can literally burst the hull. Even if the heat expansion doesn't crack a seam, the constant stress of the expansion-contraction cycle can weaken the hull.

Maintenance of modern recreational rowing boats is not the time-consuming regimen it was with traditional boats. Most of today's boats require only a few minutes' care each time you use them and a little more attention periodically. No special skills or great dedication is required—just a little time. The results in boat performance, longevity, and retained value are well worth the effort.

ROWING CLOTHES

Like the components of your boat, the clothing you wear while you row must be properly chosen and cared for to function at its peak, and to enable you to function at your peak. If your clothing is too heavy or too binding, it will inhibit you; if it's too loose, it can easily catch the oar handles at the release.

Starting at the feet, thick warm socks are important. Whether you have clogs, track shoes, or Velcro straps and plastic heel cups attached to your foot stretchers, a pair of good sweat socks will protect your feet from chafing, blisters, and cold. If you board from a beach, tuck them into your waistband, then put them on in the boat. A fresh pair of socks for each outing is a good idea, especially if you row in salt water. After the socks have soaked up the water on your feet, not to mention any that is splashed aboard during your row, they will dry with quite a bit of salt in them. This salt will attract moisture next time you wear them, and they won't be nearly as comfortable.

A common rule of thumb in rowing, as in other activities, is that knees should be covered if the temperature is below 65 degrees, but this is a matter of personal discretion. Tights, long the fashion in racing shells, are becoming more popular in recreational boats. They have the advantage of being form-fitting but not binding. The traditional attire is sweat pants, also not binding but quite a bit looser and sloppier. Select a dark color—either black or dark blue—because they will become spotted very quickly. Indelible black marks will appear on the backs of your calves where they contact the end of the tracks when you are in the layback position. For this reason, you don't want to wear your new Pierre Cardin or Halston sweat suit in the boat.

If it's warm enough to wear shorts, or you just don't like the feel of long pants and don't mind the cold, look into special rowing shorts. Rowing shorts are as important to oarsmen as bicycling shorts are to bikers. Of course, you can row in cut-off jeans, corduroy walking shorts, or your old jogging shorts, but specially designed and manufactured rowing shorts will be far better. Jeans and cords are thick and take forever to dry if they get splashed. Their seams can become a major irritant when you are sliding back and forth on a hard wooden seat, and jogging or rugby shorts, while they dry quickly, cause the same problem. The latter are also quite short and provide no protection from the sun to the upper thigh. Rowing shorts are made from quick-drying material, cover the leg to mid-thigh, and usually have a pad sewn into the seat. The padding alone can make them well worth the investment.

Your upper body, which is more susceptible to heat loss, is also more exposed—not only to wind, but to spray. If you allow yourself to become too cold, your muscles will tighten up, so warmth here is vital. Layering is preferable to wearing one or two heavy pieces of clothing, because with several layers of lighter clothing, you can peel them off as you warm up. Keep these layers tucked securely into your waistband, or you will find your hands snagging at each release. For the same reason, avoid sweat shirts with front pockets. A sweat shirt hood can also be a problem, obstructing vision if it is not cinched down tight around the head. Nevertheless, if it is cold, you will have to cover your head, because heat loss is greatest there. If a hood doesn't work for you, try a knitted watch cap. It will keep your head warm and will not impair your vision. In warm weather a billed baseball cap or visor will protect your face from the sun and your eyes from the glare.

Like your boat, your rowing wardrobe will require light maintenance. You won't want to wear the same clothes three or four times in a row without laundering them. While rowing, you will get splashed, and if you row in salt water, your clothes will become encrusted with salt, which will draw moisture out of the air. The clothes will become damp, cold, and uncomfortable. Even if you row in fresh water, your sweat will have the same effect, and it can become particularly uncomfortable under your arms and seat. It doesn't take much time or effort to care for your clothes, but you will appreciate the difference when you row, and you will see the difference in your performance.

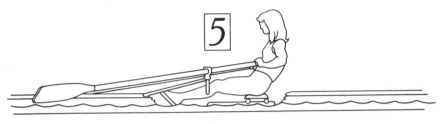

5

Safety

Safety should be your first thought whenever you set foot aboard a boat. You are venturing into an alien, often hostile environment aboard a relatively fragile craft, and there are inherent dangers. Taking the necessary precautions, however, will free you from constant concern about those dangers, allowing you to enjoy your time on the water more fully.

The two most effective safety aids cannot be mandated by the Coast Guard or any other government authority. These are knowledge and preparation, and they are your own responsibility and your best protection.

Know your own abilities and limitations, and those of your boat, and learn your local waters and the weather patterns that affect them. Understanding your limitations and those of your boat takes time. Your limitations change as you become more proficient, and what you perceive as your boat's limitations will also change. It is always best to err on the side of caution. If you harbor any doubt about your ability to make a passage, don't attempt it.

Before you start sculling, safety requires that you know how to swim. A good swimmer is more relaxed in a boat, and eventually becomes a better rower. Having a checkup before you take up a new sport is a good idea, too. Most of us put off routine checkups, so taking up sculling is a good excuse to see your physician.

WEATHER

Water and weather conditions must be studied carefully at first; later, you will learn to judge these conditions instinctively, almost subconsciously. Consider air and water temperature, wind, currents, tidal run, chop, and swell, noting how they will affect your boat and trying to predict how they may change during the course of a long row. If you have any doubts about your ability to handle existing conditions, don't go out, and in adverse but nonprohibitive conditions, lay your course wisely. For example, many oarsmen prefer to row into a headwind or against a current, tide, or chop on their way out, then turn and get the benefit of the push on the way back.

You should consider normal wind patterns in your assessment of weather conditions: Does the wind regularly switch from offshore to onshore at a given time, or does it tend to shift in a certain direction as the day wears on? When the wind changes, does it affect other conditions? Will the tides affect surface conditions? The surface may be quite smooth when tide and wind are running in the same direction, but as soon as the tide turns, a short, vicious chop may develop in some waters.

When the tide goes out, will submerged rocks become a threat? If any kind of heavy weather is predicted, assume that the weatherman is right and act accordingly. You can always deal with weather that is better than expected. Thunderstorms in particular are a threat to your safety on the water. If there is even a hint that one is approaching, don't go out.

Air and water temperatures will dictate how far from shore you venture. If either is low, you will want to be conservative, for the danger of hypothermia in the event of a capsize would be great. In extreme conditions, 150 yards offshore may be too much.

Fog is a slightly different matter. Potentially dangerous, it requires that you evaluate conditions and make choices. Knowing local weather patterns will help, but don't rely on this knowledge blindly. The fact that the fog has burned off at 1000 hours every morning during the past week does not guarantee it will burn off at 1000 on the day you plan a long row.

In all but the thickest pea soup, you will be able to see where you are going, and if you don't stray too far from familiar landmarks, you won't get lost. An onboard compass and a thorough knowledge of your area can make even longer passages reasonably safe. The real danger comes from larger craft that share the water with you. The skippers of many large boats, both power and sail, rely heavily on their radars when fog closes in. This is fine for them; they can read blips on their screens. It's not so fine for the sculler. Moving low on the water, constructed almost exclusively of fiberglass and wood, pulling boats produce very small blips on radar screens. These tiny signals are hard to distinguish from sea return caused by waves and chop. In the fog, you must row defensively—you can't rely on other boats to see you.

Fog suppresses and distorts sound, and in a thick fog a sound seems to come at you from all directions. This definitely impairs the reliability of your hearing, one of only two senses you have for detecting oncoming boats. While you may be able to see well enough to guide your boat at 5 or 6 miles per hour, remember that the powerboater traveling at four or five times that speed while staring intently at his radar screen can't see you at all. Be careful, and use your ears. If you think you hear another boat on the water, stop and make sure you know where he is and where he's going before you proceed. You can row comfortably in fog as long as you exercise extra caution.

With weather and water conditions in mind, look at your boat. Make sure everything is in good working order, and don't procrastinate in your maintenance. If a component is looser or tighter than it should be, or squeaks when it shouldn't, it isn't likely to get any better out on the water. Balancing a recreational shell a quarter-mile from shore while you try to work on your seat or oarlocks is not a good way to relax.

SAFETY EQUIPMENT

After you've made sure that your boat is in good working order, turn your attention to your equipment. A PFD (personal flotation device) is mandatory. If it won't fit into the cockpit without hampering your movements, it can be strapped to the deck, but you must have it. A bailer, securely tied to the boat, is nearly as important as the PFD. If you plan to go out before sunrise or to stay out after sunset, attach a light to your deck and carry a waterproof flashlight in the cockpit. A deck-mounted light could easily be missed by the skipper of a larger boat, but the directional beam of a flashlight can be aimed straight at him. If the weather is hot, a bottle of cool water, hat, and sun screen are important.

Your boat may be scrupulously prepared and you may have the best weather conditions possible, but the most important safety factor—you—still needs considering. How do you honestly feel? Has it been more than a week since you were last on the water? Are you stiff or sore? If you don't feel right, take it easy; the time to assess your physical condition and abilities is before you go out. If you are rowing with a more experienced sculler who wants to go farther in open water than you've gone before, and you doubt your abilities, say so. Don't allow pride to lead you into a potentially dangerous situation. If you row alone, file a "float plan." Let a responsible person know where you're going and when you expect to be back.

CAPSIZING

Should your boat capsize, your first priority will be getting back aboard. A traditional design is not likely to turn turtle, but will probably settle upright after pitching you out. She may, however, list to one side, depending on the amount of water she has taken. Her design will determine how you get back aboard, but as a general rule, you won't want to go in over the side. With no one to counterbalance your weight, the boat would probably reward such an effort by turning turtle. The best method for reboarding is over the stern, which is normally lower than the bow. Grab the stern, pull yourself up with your arms, and kick with your feet, and you should have no problem getting back aboard. Once there, you'll congratulate yourself for having tied a bailer to the boat.

If the boat does turtle, the drill will be a little different. You'll have to right it the same way a catamaran sailor rights his capsized craft—with your body weight. Maneuver the hull so it is lying beam to the wind, then swim to the leeward side. Use a knee or foot to press down on the leeward rigger, forcing the windward gunwale to rise, then grab the windward rail or rigger as you press the leeward side under, and hang your weight from the emerging side. She should flip over, spilling a lot of water in the process. As she comes upright, be careful you don't get hit by one of the sculls.

A recreational shell is more likely to turn turtle than a traditional design, but she will also be easier to right. Follow the same drill: position her beam-to, press down on the leeward rigger, and pull her over with your weight. Getting back aboard may prove more difficult, because most recreational shells have less initial stability and far less room for maneuvering in the cockpit than traditional designs. Therefore, you will probably want to come in over the bow. This will put you in the boat facing the right way, and you will avoid having to work your way around the rigging, which is usually braced aft, not forward. The procedure will be easier if the bow is pointing either dead downwind or into the eye of the wind, which reduces the boat's rolling motion. Go to the bow and pull yourself up until you are straddling the boat, as though you were riding a horse. This should be relatively easy, because your boat's fine entry won't provide much flotation, and may actually sink under your weight. Once on the bow, work your way aft quickly, keeping your legs over the side and pulling with your arms. Grip the gunwales with your hands. As your weight moves aft, the bow will rise and the boat may become slightly less stable, but having your legs in the water will help. When you reach the cockpit, straighten out the sculls and get them in the stable position before you try to put your feet in the stretchers or to do any bailing.

Practicing the capsize drill in calm, shallow water is a good idea, especially if you plan to make any open-water passages. Knowing that you can get back aboard will ease your mind when you are at sea and will help you make better decisions whenever and wherever you row.

Capsizing brings to mind another potential hazard. If your boat came with shoes instead of clogs or straps and heel cups, or if you installed shoes for added comfort and security, be sure you don't lace them too tightly. Otherwise, in the event of a capsize, you may find yourself hanging upside down like a bat in a cave. The bat, however, has two advantages: It can fly from its inverted position, and it can breathe while it hangs there.

COLLISION

Remember also that although your boat may be quite long, her mass is small. A good analogy would be a bicycle on a busy highway. In a collision, no matter whose fault it is, you lose. You are low to the water, in a place where skippers of larger boats may not be looking, so you must see them first and anticipate their movements. Get in the habit of looking over your shoulder every ten strokes or so. Since your boat is almost silent, you have the advantage of being able to hear other boats as well as see them. Powerboats can be heard from a great distance, but even a sailboat makes quite a bit of noise. The sails in the wind, the hull moving through the water, and the winches clattering all serve to warn you. When a powerboat approaches, pay attention to more than just the boat—her wake could be almost as dangerous. Get your bow around to face the oncoming wave if it's particularly steep. Then, depending upon your level of skill and your idea of what constitutes fun, you'll want either to get up some speed to meet the wave or get your oars out to balance the boat. No matter who has the right of way, be prepared to yield. Remember the bicycling analogy. A bicycle isn't going to fare very well head-on with a jeep, and neither will a sculler in an encounter with a Hatteras.

If you work at expanding your knowledge of water and weather conditions, learn to judge accurately your abilities and the situations that could affect your safety, and take time to prepare yourself and your boat, you won't have to spend much of your time on the water thinking about safety. You can't foresee every situation, but knowledge and thorough preparation can see you through almost anything.

6

Health and Rowing

There are two kinds of exercise: anaerobic and aerobic. For too many years, most people who worked out did so with anaerobic exercises, because few understood the benefits of aerobics. Anaerobic exercises are "start-stop" exercises, such as golf, tennis, handball, baseball, and football. They do not place continuous demands on the heart and lungs; instead, they require high output intermittently, allowing the body to rest at intervals. Aerobic exercise, on the other hand, places continuous demands on the body throughout the workout. Such sports as jogging, swimming, cross-country skiing, and rowing fall into the aerobic category.

THE PERFECT EXERCISE

In addition to being an aerobic exercise, rowing offers benefits that most other sports do not. Rowing is not an age-dependent sport—you can start rowing long before you can legally drive, and you can continue to enjoy it well into your eighties. Rowing does not have a high injury rate, either from contact (such as in football) or from punishing of the joints (as in jogging). It is a complete exercise, working the entire body, so you do not have to complement your rowing program with any other exercises. Sliding-seat rowing burns approximately twice as many calories as jogging can in a given period of time, and it puts you on the water, which for many rowers is the main attraction of the sport. Instead of dodging traffic and breathing exhaust fumes, you glide over the surface of a lake, river, or bay, enjoying the immeasurable psychological benefits of the activity while working every major muscle group in your body.

Frederick C. Hagerman, Chairman of the Department of Zoology and Microbiology at Ohio University, wrote an article entitled "Rowing for Your Health," published in *Rowing* USA's August-September 1982 issue, from which I quote. "Intensity (of exercise) need not be exceedingly high in order for the healthy individual to benefit from rowing; exercising at 65 to 75 percent of maximal work output is sufficient to elicit a training response that can be regulated by utilizing a target heart rate. Maximal heart rate can be estimated by the simple formula of 220 – age; a target heart rate for the desired percent of maximum can be calculated using the following formula: percent of maximum desired × (maximum heart rate – resting heart rate) + resting heart rate. For example, if a 30-year-old person with a resting heart rate of 70 beats per minute wants to work at 70 percent of his maximum heart rate, then 220 – 30 = 190, and .70 (190 – 70) + 70 = 154, the target heart rate. Thus, a heart rate of 154 should be maintained for the duration of the exercise if the desired training stimulus is to be achieved."

To realize the maximum benefit from rowing, you will need to do steady-state, long-distance workouts on a regular basis. According to Hagerman, "The duration and frequency of exercise are probably the two most important factors for improving physical fitness. The beginning exerciser should strive to exercise at least 15 minutes, working up to 30 to 45 minutes after 8 to 10 weeks of regular aerobic exercise. It is best to exercise at least four days per week, with the exercise bouts spread evenly over a seven-day period. If this schedule can be increased to five to six days per week, results are even better. It must be remembered that duration and regularity are very important and that rate of work or intensity should be kept well below maximal levels. In this way, a person can maintain adequate physical fitness and, at the same time, keep fatigue and injuries to a minimum."

Discussing the physiological benefits of rowing, Hagerman continues, "The ability to take in, deliver, and use oxygen is probably the best measure of physical fitness. Rowing and sculling on a regular basis seem to be among the most potent stimuli for increasing oxygen consumption. Oxygen transport is largely dependent on the cardiac output, or the heart's ability to deliver blood, and is defined as the product of heart rate (number of beats per minute) times stroke volume (amount of blood ejected by heart with each beat). Numerically, cardiac output at rest is approximately 5 liters per minute and can be increased by elite oarsmen to nine times this value during maximal rowing efforts.

"An individual beginning a regular sculling program might expect the resting heart rate to decrease significantly after a period of four to six weeks. This is because the heart muscle is accommodating gradually to the increased workload, and, as a result, stroke volume increases. Since the conditioned heart can now deliver a larger volume of blood with each beat, it can become less rate-dependent and thus more efficient. It is not uncommon for the resting heart rate to drop from an average of 75 beats per minute to 55 beats per minute after some weeks of regular aerobic exercise. At the same time, stroke volume is increasing. Because the resting heart rate usually declines over time, it is important to monitor this rate regularly and readjust the target training heart rate upward accordingly to maintain the training stimulus."

We now know that a workout program, no matter how well thought out and how rigorously adhered to, is only as good as the fuel we give our bodies. Exercise and nutrition must complement each other. This book is about rowing, not nutrition, but it would be incomplete if it did not briefly address this subject. Patricia Ingram, M.S., R.D., has written an essay on "Food as Fuel," which appears as Appendix 1 of this book. Appendix 2 contains some of her suggestions for further reading on nutrition. New books on the subjects of nutrition, health, and sports performance appear regularly, so check with your local library or bookstore for the latest titles. If you decide to change your diet radically, check with your doctor first.

THE RIGHT WORKOUT FOR YOU

Whatever motivates you to row—the need for a fitness program, the love of racing, or the desire to get out on the water—you'll want to take full advantage of the time you spend in the boat. To do this, you'll need to structure your on-the-water time. You will gain far more from a planned workout than from just going out and rowing. Even if you have no interest in racing and the phrase "fitness program" is repugnant to you, you will benefit from a planned rowing schedule.

Before getting in the boat, you should do some stretching (including at least the two stretches discussed later in this chapter). Once you're in the boat, you will want to warm up gradually. Don't leave the beach or dock at full pressure. Row for 10 to 15 minutes at quarter- and half-pressure. If you choose to start with one of the drills discussed in Chapter 3, no-leg or no-feather rowing, that's great, but don't count it as part of your warm-up time. Your warm up should consist of full-stroke rowing—5 to 7 minutes at quarter-pressure, and an equal·time at half-pressure. Once you're warmed up, there are several ways to improve your rowing, but they all have two things in common: heart rate and duration.

You won't want to do exactly the same workout each day. There are two reasons for this. First, you'll "plateau out" and stop gaining at the same rate. Second, you'll get bored in the long run and lose interest. After all, how many times can you row the same course and retain your enthusiasm?

There are different routines you can use to keep your interest up while achieving maximum fitness. You can do a long-distance row (say, 12 miles) once a week and two or three hour-long rows the other times you go out. If a long row doesn't appeal to you, you can do different drills during your regular hour-long rows.

Rather than rowing from point A to point B and back, or doing laps around a given course, you can row pyramids. Pyramids can be based either on time or on number of strokes. In both forms, pyramiding is a useful technique—it keeps the mind occupied while it builds the body. To do "time" pyramids, warm up, do one minute of three-quarter-pressure strokes, then one minute at quarter-pressure, then two minutes at three-quarter-pressure, and two minutes at quarter-pressure, progressing up to four or five minutes. Then work your way back down the same pyramid. Going up to five minutes and back in this way will result in a sustained workout of 50 minutes. To do "stroke" pyramids, start with 10 strokes at three-quarter-pressure, then 10 at quarter-pressure, move up to 20 at three-quarter-pressure and 20 at quarter-pressure, and so on up and down the pyramid. These pyramids will have the effect of a steady-state, long-distance workout because the light-work period they include is not long enough for a full recovery. You can easily develop pyramids to suit your own needs.

If speed is your goal, interval work will be better for you than pyramids. Intervals involve getting your heart rate back down under 100 beats per minute before the next high-pressure piece. For instance, if you do a minute at three-quarter-pressure or higher, you will need 3 to 3½ minutes of slow, easy paddling to get your rate down before the next pressure piece. The better your condition, the sooner your heart rate will drop, but a 1:3 pressure-to-rest ratio is a good place to start. As with pyramids or any other technique, a conscientious warm-up period is essential for interval training.

Some recreational rowers, iconoclasts by nature, shun any kind of structured workout. They're on the water to row, not to count strokes or take pulse rates. Some rowers train by balancing speed against endurance for an hour at a time. They go out and row for an hour, making a note of the distance covered. The next time out, they try to go farther in the same hour. This kind of workout works best for those who are inclined toward long-distance racing.

STAYING IN SHAPE

While rowing is a complete exercise, you must practice it regularly to get any real benefit from it. If you were a runner and did nothing all week—no running, no exercises, no stretching—you wouldn't expect to go out on Sunday and run five miles without paying for it later. Rowing is no different. If you can get out on the water only one day a week, you are going to be miserable afterward unless you stay in shape the rest of the time. You may enjoy rowing so much that you are on the water five or six times a week, or you may want to race, but you will still find exercising and stretching important. If your climate does not permit year-round rowing, you will need some form of exercise during the winter so you won't suffer badly when you start rowing in the spring. All the exercises discussed here are as valuable to the once-a-week rower as they are to the competitive sculler.

Any stretching you do as part of your exercise program will help your rowing, but stretches borrowed from running and gymnastics can be particularly helpful. Whatever else you do, there are two stretches you should definitely include in your exercise program. The first of these will stretch your hamstrings, which are vital to getting the proper forward lean during the recovery. As we saw in Chapter 3, if you can't get enough forward angle, you limit your reach at the catch and shorten the arc of your stroke. Stand with your feet together and bend at the waist, letting your arms drop and keeping your legs straight. Don't "bounce" to get your hands closer to the floor, just hang. The longer you hold this, the better, but don't force it. The second stretch will work on your back, important both to your lean-forward at the catch and, to a lesser extent, your layback at the release. Lie on your back and swing your legs over your head so that your knees flank your head. You may have to support your hips with your hands when you first do this exercise. As with the first stretch, don't force it, just let your body stretch into the position.

There are some sports complementary to sculling that you can practice in the off season to keep in shape. If you are in training for competition, they can increase your stamina and strength. As long as your shins and knees are in good shape, running can be beneficial. As an aerobic exercise, running will build up your capacity for long-distance rowing. Cycling is also good—many racing scullers cross-train on bikes. If you live in a cold climate, indoor cycling on a trainer is a great winter exercise. Swimming is also a good, compatible exercise, but you will find it harder to get your heart rate up.

Perhaps running three to five miles a day doesn't appeal to you, you don't want to spend the money on a bicycle, and swimming isn't possible or desirable. There is another exercise for you—running stairs. This is a great workout, takes almost no time, and can be done nearly anywhere. A few minutes spent running stairs provides as much benefit as a much longer time spent running on the flat.

The 22-Minute Drill

If you enjoy working with weights, there is a workout called the "22-Minute Drill" you can do. It works your respiratory system and increases your strength. Do this drill with free weights, not machines, because you want the extra benefit of improving your coordination, balance, and timing. It also works your opposing muscles, keeping them strong to prevent injury. With a bar and some weights, you can do this drill at home in a short period of time. It doesn't require a trip to the gym or hours of your time.

The 22-Minute Drill consists of seven exercises. Each exercise is repeated 10 times, and the entire cycle is repeated six times, all within 22 minutes. When you start, you will want to be conservative about the weight you load on the bar. The drill will make you sore, even though it doesn't feel like it at first, so start light. An average-size man will start at about 40 pounds, but if you have no weight-lifting experience or feel that 40 pounds is a little heavy for you, go down to 30. In the beginning, repeat the cycle only three times, because, like sculling, the 22-Minute Drill is something you must work your way into. No matter how long you've been on the program, don't do the drill more than three times a week.

After you do some stretches to limber up, check the clock and start the drill with the power clean. Start with the bar at your ankles, not touching the ground, knees bent, butt tucked under, and head up. Push up with your legs, then with your back, and your arms will carry the bar to your chin. Then slowly lower the bar back to your ankles. This exercise is directly related to rowing and works your legs, back, and arms.

After 10 repetitions of the power clean, move to bent-over rows. With your legs straight but not locked, lean over so that the bar hangs toward the ground from straight arms. Keeping your legs and back straight, lift the bar 10 times. Bent-over rows work your lats and your lower back.

The third exercise, the snatch, starts with the bar on the ground, the only time the bar should touch the ground during a cycle. You will bend your legs, pick up the bar, then thrust with your legs and straighten your back—the arms will finally put the bar over your head. Along with working your legs, back, and arms, the snatch will improve your coordination and balance more than any other exercise in the drill.

After 10 repetitions of the snatch, move to the squats. Place the bar behind your head, resting it on your shoulders. With your back straight and head up, bend your knees to about 90 degrees, then straighten your legs. This is like doing deep-knee bends with weights on your shoulders, but don't bend your knees past 90 degrees. The squats exercise the quadriceps (the big muscles of the legs), the hamstrings, and the gluteus maximus.

Dead lifts come next. With the bar in front of you and your legs straight, bend at the waist and let the bar hang from your arms. When the bar is just off the floor, straighten up, using just your back. This will work your lower back.

After 10 dead lifts comes the military press. Start with the bar at your shoulders, wrists bent, then push up. Bring the bar back down below your chin, then push up again. The military press works your pectorals and biceps.

Finally, do 10 curls. You can either keep the same grip you've been using throughout the drill and do "French curls," or reverse the grip for more common curls. Whichever grip you choose, start with the bar at your waist and lift it to your chest, bending your arms at the elbows and keeping them right against the sides of your body. French curls will work the triceps and muscles of your forearms, while the regular curls will work your biceps. That is the full drill, and it should be completed in 22 minutes.

In the beginning, once you've worked your way up to 10 of each exercise and six full cycles, it's time to start paying attention to the time the drill takes. If you can run through the whole drill in less than 22 minutes, it's time to increase the weight. Add weight in small increments, 5 pounds at a time, so that you don't strain yourself. The 22-Minute Drill is hard work, but doing it regularly will make you a better rower.

Rowing is a thorough exercise, but more than that, it is enjoyable for its own sake. It is not merely a path to the goal of fitness, and its rewards are not limited to the physical benefits of the exercise.

Women and Rowing

Women are attracted to rowing for the same reasons that men are. They have the same goals—physical and mental well-being—and the benefits of a complete exercise program are not lost on modern women any more than they are on men. Times have changed, and so have women's ideals of beauty. It is desirable now to appear physically fit, and fashion has followed this shift in outlook. Clothes emphasize the new look, and it is okay for a woman to be strong and capable.

Rowing may be the perfect sport for women. They seem to adapt to it faster than men, and rowing accommodates different levels of skill and interest, which can be particularly appealing to women. At the recreational level, sculling is a relaxed, friendly sport. The only person you compete against is yourself. If a woman wants to compete, she will compete against other women. She can train at her own pace, without overexerting herself. At the competitive level, American women have become such a power in the sport of rowing that in the 1984 Olympics the U.S. women did better than the men.

Rowing was once a strength and "arms" sport, but contrary to myth, it no longer is. Before Arthur Martin introduced sliding-seat rowing to the masses, the recreational rower had to choose a dory, peapod, or similar fixed-seat design. Rowing these boats was a task better suited to a man's upper body than a woman's. Today, the reality behind the myth is dead, and the myth is quickly dying. Women are finding their niche in rowing, to the benefit of both themselves and the sport.

Even though women take to the technique of sliding-seat rowing faster than men, they are still at a disadvantage when it comes to getting their boats to and from the water. At first glance, moving a 22-foot boat that weighs more than 60 pounds may seem difficult to a woman. If she wants to be independent, not having to rely on the help of a friend each time she wishes to go rowing, a woman will have to learn to compensate for her lack of brute strength. All that is required is a little ingenuity and forethought. In Chapter 1, we discussed the use of a small cart for moving a boat about onshore. A cart is almost indispensable for a woman who doesn't want to depend on others each time she goes rowing. One or two experiments with a boat and cart will show her the best way to deal with her particular setup, but here are some suggestions for using a cart to full advantage.

If you are lucky enough to live near the water or to have the use of a boathouse, your boat could be stored on the cart. If the boat can't be kept on the cart and either hangs from the rafters or is stored on a rack, it will be an easy matter to shift it to the cart to be rolled out to the beach or dock. If you hang the boat from the rafters, you can place the cart under a balance point and lower the boat onto it. If you keep the boat on a rack, it will take just a little more effort to get her onto the cart. Pull either the bow or the stern off the rack and set it on the floor, using a towel to prevent scratching the gelcoat. Then lift the other end off the rack and pivot the boat so that it rests on the cart. With this method, you will never have to lift the full weight of the boat. To get the boat back on the rack, simply reverse the process.

Getting the boat on and off a car is just like getting her on and off a rack. Again, use the cart to move the boat—always let the ground or the car rack take at least half the boat's weight. Roll the boat up to the car so that the bow is well forward of the rear rack. Put a towel under the stern to prevent scratching, then lift the bow, and swing it up onto the rack. Once the bow is resting on the rear rack, go to the stern, and slide the boat up into position. To take the boat off the car, reverse the process.

At the water, roll the cart down the beach so that the bow is in the water. Rest the bow on the bottom, and lift the stern off the cart. This way you won't have to slide the boat far across the sand. If you launch from a dock, all you have to do is let the boat slide off the cart and into the water, but be sure to tie a leash to the stern so she doesn't drift away.

When you are retrieving the boat from shallow water, it is a good idea to put the cart as close to the water as possible. If the cart is rustproof, you can even roll it partway in. Having as much water as possible under the stern will prevent its dragging on the bottom and either scratching the gelcoat or bending the fin. If you can, lift the boat with an incoming surge, which will put a little more water under the stern. The wake of a passing boat will help—you don't need a wave of major proportions.

If you don't have far to move your boat and the terrain is relatively level, you could get by with something lighter and less bulky than a cart. Inflatable rollers, or even fenders from a large pleasure boat, can be used to roll your boat in and out of a boathouse or along a beach. Rollers are lighter and easier to store than a cart.

Most coaches say that their women students ask three questions when they start rowing. They want to know how much strength rowing requires, how to move a boat to and from the water, and how rowing will affect their bodies. We have already dealt with the myth that rowing requires massive amounts of upper-body strength, and we have shown that with a cart or rollers, a woman can row whenever and wherever she chooses.

One question remains: What effect will sculling have on a woman's body? There is no simple answer. In order to describe the changes a woman may expect when she takes up rowing, we assume that she is going to invest a reasonable amount of time in the sport—say, at least three one-hour rows per week. At first, she will feel sore—the satisfying soreness of muscles that have been used, not the pain of flesh that has been abused. She will be using muscles she probably hasn't used before. Soreness in the abdominal muscles and the lats (latissimus dorsi) means she is developing the proper technique. Soreness in the lower back is an indication of poor technique.

As a woman rows, her muscle tone will improve, most noticeably in the arms and legs. She will not develop the muscular look of a man. Her weight will redistribute, with muscle replacing some of her body fat. Because muscle is heavier and denser than fat, she may actually gain weight while her dress size drops. In general, rowing will help a woman develop upper-body strength and muscle tone.

Many doctors now recognize that exercising during pregnancy is beneficial to both mother and child. Rowing is perfect for the pregnant woman. Since the weight of the body is supported by the boat and there is no vertical motion, there is no stress on either the stomach or the breasts. Therefore, rowing will not cause or accentuate stretch marks as other sports might. For the same reasons, a pregnant woman would not be putting added stress on her joints, as she would with jogging. Rowing gives her all the advantages of exercise, without the strains. If a woman has been rowing before she becomes pregnant, there is no reason for her to stop unless her doctor advises her to do so.

If a woman chooses to compete, she can enter either traditional sculling races, where she will race against other women, or recreational races, where she will race in a woman's class inside the larger race. If she chooses the long-distance recreational races, she may find that she does quite well against the men's class. Since rowing is essentially a "leg" sport, women are on an equal basis with men where the primary muscle group is concerned. If a man and woman are in the same physical condition and are of the same size, their legs will be equally strong. The second most important muscle group in rowing is the lats. Here again, a woman is as strong as a man of equal size and fitness. A woman is weaker only in the third most important area—the arms. Women compensate for this disadvantage by having an extra layer of fat. This fat stores substantial amounts of glycogen, which turns into simple sugar as the body demands it, giving women extra stamina and endurance.

Once women overcome the initial hurdles, they tend to become hooked on rowing. They will enjoy the benefits of an overall fitness program, rather than the localized exercise of sports such as jogging. All women who row will be awakened to the beauty, pleasure, and camaraderie of the sport. Once a male-dominated sport, sculling has proved it has something to offer anyone, regardless of age or gender. Women are coming to it in numbers greater than ever before. Both women and rowing are the better for it.

Where Can Recreational Rowing Take You?

As a lifelong sport, sculling can't be beaten. If chosen and cared for properly, your first boat can last a lifetime. The same craft you bought as a beginner will still give you hours and hours of enjoyable, healthful exercise 30 years later. Of course, we all change with time, and what we want from our chosen sport may change, too.

Many people take up rowing as a way to get into shape, only to find that the means becomes an end in itself. The thrill of rowing—blending one long, powerful stroke with each successive one—supersedes the benefits of the exercise. The more you row, the more you want to row, and the more you expect from rowing.

After some time, you may decide you want to explore aspects of the sport that you were not interested in or aware of before. This desire to advance means you will want a "better" boat, which usually translates as "faster" or "bigger." After becoming comfortable in their recreational boats, many rowers want to try their hand at racing, while others find long-distance rowing intriguing.

If you should decide you need a "better" boat, go back and review all the reasons for which you chose your first one. Many of them, especially the logistical considerations, will probably still be valid, and should be kept in mind along with your new goals. Many of the boats you perused at the time of your first purchase will deserve a second look, and there will be new ones to examine and row. Your first boat will have been an invaluable learning experience, and should make buying your second one much easier. You will also find that your second boat does not involve as great a financial burden as the first. Recreational rowing boats do not depreciate greatly; selling your first boat should go a long way toward paying for your second.

RACING THE RECREATIONAL BOAT

If you decide to try your hand at racing, you may not have to change boats, at least not at first. Traditional rowing clubs, where true racing shells have always dominated, have yielded to pressure and have finally begun offering heats for recreational boats. Frequently, they offer starts for one-design classes, if there are enough boats of a single design to warrant it, and for open classes. Placement in open classes is usually determined by the length and beam of the boats entered, and frequently one design or another will be favored by the luck of the draw. To the novice racer, however, this is not terribly important. In the beginning, you are there to gain experience, not to win races. Recreational races staged by traditional clubs are usually run over the same course the club uses for its shells, so they are short, straight-line affairs on glass-smooth water. As an introduction to formal racing, this type of event can turn out to be a great learning experience. Racing in several events over a period of time will show you how your boat-handling skills, speed, and strength have progressed.

Any kind of racing will require that you develop new skills. If you plan to become involved in the very structured, formal world of traditional sculling races, it would be wise to meet with the sponsoring club's rowing coordinators, coach, or race committee chairman to learn how the race is organized before you go out on the water.

Whether you're lining up in lanes to do a 2,000-meter sprint or jockeying for position behind a long line to start a 10-mile, open-ocean race, your starting technique will be similar. At the start, you will take four to six quick strokes with your arms only. Although they are considerably weaker than legs, arms are much faster. These "arms only" strokes serve to break the inertia and get the boat moving. In a lightweight shell, use fewer of these strokes; in a heavier recreational boat, use more. Once the boat starts to respond, begin to lengthen the stroke, going first to a half-slide, then to a three-quarter, and finally to a full slide. As soon as you've lengthened to a full stroke, pour on a solid power-20 before settling down to a lower stroke rate. Your pace for most of the race will depend on the type of boat you're racing, the length of the course, and your skill and stamina. For a recreational boat in a distance race, 22 strokes per minute is a good figure to start with; in a shell, the distance will be shorter and the rate higher.

Steering in a race is a little different from routine steering, in that you can't break stroke to pull hard on one oar or the other. Instead, you must learn to turn by increasing the arc of one oar. If you're leaving a mark of the course to starboard, you will need to lengthen the stroke of your port-side oar. These will be gradual turns, not spin turns. Extend the reach of your right hand for a couple of strokes, and feel the bow begin to turn. Depending on the radius of the turn, you may want to even up the stroke for two more pulls, then reach out with your right hand again. It will take practice to learn to hit your apex, but it will come. Your turns will be wide, but you won't scrub off speed, and you will keep a good, even stroke rate throughout.

As the race nears its end, you will need to evaluate the competition. Don't let a competitor draw you into a sprint to the finish if you're not ready for it. He could make his sprint too early and fade at the finish, dragging you down with him. Row your own race, know when you want to make the kick for the finish, and do it then.

If you think traditional shell racing is your goal, racing a recreational boat is a good way to find out. Spending time at regattas will also allow you to get to know some of the members of your local club and see what the club has to offer. After several races, if you still want to race shells, you should join the club that best suits your needs. Most clubs have coaches, seminars, and club-owned trainers and shells for the use of their members. As a member, you can avail yourself of these coaching services and soon be racing in a trainer, all at minimal cost.

Trainers

The trainer is a logical intermediate step between a recreational boat and a true racing shell. Trainers are longer, lighter, and narrower than recreational boats, and therefore considerably faster and less stable, though not nearly as fast or unstable as a racing shell. The first time you sit in one, you will probably feel as if you had never rowed sliding-seat before. A trainer will force you to refine the skills you learned in your first boat. Clean blade work, a controlled slide, and smooth, constant application of power become even more important.

Just getting aboard a trainer calls for a level of skill that most recreational boats do not require. Learning the technique will stand you in good stead when you move up to a racing shell. Trainers are built heavily enough so that you won't put your foot through the bottom if you step in the wrong place, but the same cannot be said of racing shells. The wrong step in a shell can be very expensive, and the experience you gain in a trainer can save you not only money, but also a great deal of inconvenience and embarrassment.

Getting aboard a trainer or racing shell is much like boarding a recreational boat, but it requires more finesse and balance. Before attempting it, you should review pages 36–40. In your recreational boat, your technique has probably become a bit sloppy, as you tend to rely on the stability of the boat rather than perfect form. You will find boarding a trainer from a beach far easier than boarding from a dock.

Start by pushing the seat way forward to the release position. After you have squared the sculls to the hull and are sure the blades are flat on the water, you will want to keep a firmer grip on the oars than you may have become used to doing. The hand gripping the shore-side rigger should be prepared to give a little more lift than it would with a recreational boat. Step directly onto the foot deck with one foot while you balance the boat with the sculls and lift with the hand on the rigger. Support yourself with that foot and swing your other foot up and directly down into the stretchers. Pretend you are aboard a shell and *do not* step into the bottom of the boat. With your foot in the stretcher, ease down into the seat, then slip the other foot into the stretcher. Though it is possible to board a trainer in shallow water by straddling it, sitting down, and then pulling your legs in, as you would with your recreational boat, this method is not recommended. A trainer is designed to prepare you for a racing shell, and racing shells should not be boarded by straddling. The cockpit of a racing shell is surrounded by a splash box, which is very lightly constructed. Straddling a shell and swinging your legs in can easily result in damage to the splash box.

You board a trainer from a dock the same way you would a recreational boat, but with the same precautions you observe when boarding from the beach. The first time you get into a trainer, from a beach or a dock, it is advisable to have someone spot for you, standing by to hold a rigger for extra balance.

It will probably take three or four outings in a trainer before you feel as comfortable in it as you do in your recreational boat. If you've decided you want to race a shell, the time so spent will be invaluable. Most traditional clubs race trainers regularly, and rowing several heats in one of these events will teach you a great deal. Without trainers, the transition from recreational boat to racing shell would be difficult.

The Racing Shell

In a shell, you refine your skills even more, although you may feel you're taking two steps backward. All the unease you felt the first time you sat in a recreational boat or a trainer will return. Once more, each flaw in your stroke or balance will be magnified. Even though you may never have dumped either a recreational boat or trainer, don't be surprised if you find yourself swimming the first or second time you take out a shell. It happens a lot—it's nothing to be ashamed of.

If you do take a spill, you must either get back into the boat or get the boat and yourself back to shore. For the good of the boat, the latter is preferable. Of course, if you are far from shore or in very cold water, your safety comes before anything else. If you can *safely* swim and tow the boat to shore, or grab the stern of another sculler's shell and be pulled back to the beach, do it. As soon as you reach shore, empty the shell and immediately reboard. It is important to analyze the reasons for the spill, but don't dwell on the accident and lose your confidence.

If you are far from shore, or if the water is dangerously cold, you'll have to get back aboard or at least out of the water. First, you must right the boat. Even though you are in the water and have no leverage, this shouldn't be a problem—the boat is light and has positive flotation. Simply grab an oarlock and push up; the turtled shell should come upright. In the process, a lot of the water in the cockpit will spill out. Once the boat is floating right side up, you will need to straighten out the sculls. Square them to the boat with the blades flat on the water, just as if you were boarding from a beach. Grip the handles with one hand, and the oars will stabilize the shell. Place your other hand on the foot deck, push down hard and give a strong kick with your feet. As your body lifts, swing a leg over the boat so that you are straddling it. Without letting go of the oars, fix yourself in the seat and swing your legs over the splash box and into the stretchers. Boarding the boat in this manner may crack or break the splash box, but this can be repaired. Your safety comes first. Don't worry about the small amount of water that will be left in the boat, just row back to shore and safety.

It is very unlikely that you would be unable to reboard your swamped boat in the manner just described, but if you can't, the boat can still provide positive flotation and keep you out of the cold water. With the boat upright, use the riggers to pull yourself up. Keep as much of your body as possible out of the water—hypothermia is your worst enemy in cold water. Lying on top of the boat will keep you warmer and make you more visible. The Red Cross and Coast Guard both advise you to "never leave your boat," and this book can only repeat their advice. None of this should scare you away from shells. They are hard to master, but well worth the effort.

After you have rowed a club-owned shell in a few races, you may decide it's time to buy one. Like all high-performance racing equipment, a shell reacts to the subtlest changes in tuning, and minor changes in oarlock pitch or height will make a major difference in how the boat feels. As your skill improves, you will become more sensitive to each such change, and before rowing the club's shell you will have to spend considerable time retuning it to suit your own body and style. Owning a boat will obviate the need for constant retuning and allow you to row anytime. If you decide you must have a shell, be prepared to pay heavily for the privilege of joining rowing's elite. Racing shells cost upward of $2,500 and also require more specialized maintenance. On the other hand, rowing offers no purer thrill than pulling across mirror-smooth water in a racing shell.

RECREATIONAL BOAT REGATTAS

If you have done a few heats down the lanes in your recreational boat and have decided that straight-line sprint racing is not for you though you still want to improve your rowing, there are other areas to investigate. Many builders and some dealers frequently stage one-design regattas and rowing seminars for the owners of their boats. These are usually less formal events than traditional rowing club regattas. Typically, they are off-the-beach regattas with races from point to point or around a convenient landmark, such as an island or buoy. They tend to be longer than the traditional sprints and are run in less protected waters.

The one-design regattas and seminars attract scullers whose skills and backgrounds vary widely. While you will meet some hard-core racers at these events, the competition is usually less intense than it is at traditional rowing club regattas. The focus of dealer- and builder-sponsored regattas is usually on learning and fun, rather than strictly on competition.

With the rising interest in recreational rowing, a new form of rowing club has emerged to fill the needs of scullers that the traditional clubs do not meet. This new breed of rowing club is usually smaller and does not always offer the facilities of the older, more established clubs. While some do have boathouses, club-owned boats, coaches, and seminars, many of these clubs have only a small core membership. What they lack in tradition and facilities, they more than make up for in the enthusiasm of their members.

Rather than the traditional sprints, the new genre of rowing club stages longer races designed to challenge recreational boats. Normally, the regattas are open events, allowing you to "run what you brung." This means you can compete in your present boat as long as you like or until you decide you want something "better." Many of the clubs have one or two designs that are popular among the members, and those designs may race as a class within the larger regatta. Many scullers use these events to compete with a particular individual or to measure their personal progress. The races are structured loosely enough to accommodate the needs of any recreational sculler.

The longer races of the new clubs, anywhere from 3 to 30 miles, are held in a variety of conditions, but most are staged on open water. As with the races staged by builders and dealers, usually both a long and short course are offered, and a cruising class is frequently an option. A sculler new to racing can choose the short course or cruise over the same waters in company with others, while the hard-core racers go for the long course. Most of these events include a post-race picnic, which gives the less experienced scullers a chance to mix with the pros. The experienced scullers are usually proud to show off their

An Aero and a Vancouver 21 racing in the shadow of San Francisco's Golden Gate Bridge.

boats and let other people row them. A new club member can often find himself rowing two or three different boats the afternoon after a race.

While these clubs are relatively new, many of their regattas have already become classics. In the Pacific Northwest, there is the Great Cross Sound Race; in Newport, Rhode Island, the Small Boat Rowing Race; in the High Sierras, there is the Lake Tahoe North Shore Regatta; and in Southern California, the ultra-marathon of rowing races, the Catalina–Marina del Rey Race. In the San Francisco Bay area, a recreational rower could race nearly every weekend from early spring to late fall. The new rowing clubs are appearing everywhere there is water, and they offer increasing numbers of races and cruises.

Racing Safety

These longer, open-water races differ from the traditional club regattas not only in structure, but also in the demands they place on individual entrants. At a sprint race, you can see the entire course just by turning your head, and you know the water is calm or the shells wouldn't be out there. That's not the case at a recreational event. Even though you will be racing or cruising in the company of others and support boats may be supplied, you are ultimately responsible for your own safety. Although your recreational boat is more stable than a shell, you will be competing in rougher water. You will also be farther from shore for a longer time than you ever would be in a shell

A triple finishing the Catalina–Marina del Rey Race.

or during training in your own boat. Accurate, informed judgment of your abilities and the conditions you face becomes increasingly important as the races lengthen.

You, and only you, will decide what is safe to attempt. Before a race, it will be your responsibility to check on weather and sea conditions, both for the start of the race and for the rest of the day. You will need to know about expected wind direction and velocity, surf and currents along the course, the state of the tides, and rain or thunderstorm predictions. Remember, just because "everyone else is going" doesn't mean you have to—it's entirely up to you.

Even though the cockpit of your recreational boat is small, there are a few things you will want to take with you when you race or cruise over a long course. At the very least, you will need a PFD, bailer, water bottle, and towing line. You may also need protection from the sun. A

An Alden Single in rough going, conditions in which these boats revel.

A trainer being rowed in rough conditions. More shell-like than the Alden Single, this trainer's bow is completely underwater, and the boat is threatening to broach. Only an experienced sculler can handle a boat like this in these conditions.

hat, shirt, and strong sun block will prevent a lot of discomfort in the short run and may protect you from skin cancer in the long run.

Modifying Your Boat for Racing

If you find you enjoy recreational racing, consider making some minor modifications to your boat. A couple of inexpensive additions can make your boat much more comfortable and efficient in these events. A compass is invaluable, not just in getting from point A to point B, but in keeping a straight course and conserving the energy that weaving all over the water saps away. Since you are facing aft and most compasses are manufactured to be read facing forward, the direction you read will be 180 degrees off your heading. Back-facing compasses are hard to find, so most scullers simply learn to convert the figures in their heads. If you have to make several changes in course over the length of the race, you might plot the compass headings before you start, convert them, and tape a list of headings in the boat.

The more people race, the greater the number of water-bottle mounts one sees in their boats. Rather than have extra water bottles rolling around under their seats, racers buy bicycle water bottles with lightweight aluminum cages and mount them in a convenient location. That way, they can take a drink without having to grope around for the bottle first. Stopwatches and real-time watches also show up regularly on recreational racing boats. Scullers use them to keep stroke counts and pace themselves.

Comfort becomes more important as the distances covered in your outings increase. Fine-tuning the rig will greatly enhance your comfort. (See Chapter 4.) Since you contact the boat in only two places, at your seat and at your feet, changes in these areas will be especially significant.

By the time you get to this stage, you will probably have become just as accustomed to the tiny wooden seat as a bicyclist is to his hard narrow seat. If the seat still bothers you, a thin pad could make a big difference, but remember, if you make a significant change in the height of your seat, you will need to retune your rigging to compensate.

Recreational boats come with a variety of foot-stretcher arrangements. Some builders supply leather clogs, while others supply straps that are held in place by Velcro and plastic heel cups. After some time in their boats, many recreational scullers take a hint from shell racers and replace their clogs or straps and heel cups with track shoes. Having your feet in a pair of shoes can give you a good, solid feeling in the boat; it can also save your feet from chafing against leather or straps. There are some things you'll need to know about mounting shoes in the place of builder-supplied equipment. They can easily be bolted by drilling through the cleat inserts and then using a stainless steel, flat-head machine bolt pushed through from

An example of customized stretchers. Track shoes have replaced heel cups and straps, and a watch with a stopwatch function has been laced into the shoes. Three bicycle water-bottle cages have been mounted on a marine plywood shelf, and a bailer and a compass have been added.

the inside. The bolt will be sucked down as the nut is tightened, and the head will snug up against the cleat insert. The head of the bolt will be below the inner sole of the shoe, where the sculler won't feel it. The heels should not be bolted down, so that they can lift at the catch; they should, however, be loosely tied in place, so that if you spill the boat, they will stay in position and your feet will slip out. For the same reason, you should never tie yourself in too tightly.

Some scullers get so high-tech that their foot blocks tend to look more like the cockpits of small planes than rowing boats. Digital stroke meters, knotmeters, and compasses with liquid crystal displays have found their way aboard recreational racers. A variety of complex timing devices incorporating real-time, time-from-start, and stopwatch functions have proliferated and can either be mounted on the foot blocks or woven into the laces of the shoes. Suction-style bailers, similar to those used on Olympic-class racing dinghies, have been installed in cockpits so that bailing becomes an automatic function of speed through water.

After making some additions or modifications to their boats, many

A *performance-oriented, high-tech stretcher arrangement incorporating a digital compass, knot meter, stroke meter, and time from start and real time watches.*

scullers find that they don't need to buy a "better" boat. On the other hand, if you want to be the first to finish on the long course, rowing these races will give you a chance to learn from more experienced scullers and see what kind of boats they're rowing. A few of the most competitive scullers may be rowing custom boats, but most of them will be rowing boats that don't cost much more than the average recreational boat. They will be in the boats on the lower righthand side of Gordie Nash's chart—the ARS, California Wherry, and Vancouver 21.

CRUISING

If you've tried a couple of these races and decided that they're not for you, but you did enjoy the atmosphere, you might try joining with

A pair of modern recreational shells. On the right, the stripped-down Aero, 21 feet long and just 40 pounds. On the left, the Vancouver 21, the same hull with a splashbox, which adds 8 pounds but considerable security and dryness.

those who cruise the course or becoming involved with a cruise that is planned separately from a race. Cruising is more like going for a row with friends than racing. Instead of speeding past small inlets on the most direct course, you can take the time to explore as you go. This is what recreational boats were really designed and built for. They take well to choppy water and are not affected by ground swells or waves reflected off rocks. They are maneuverable, turning easily in their own length, and most are tough enough to be beached on a sandy stretch so that you can get out and explore.

All the precautions needed for long-distance, open-water races also apply to long-distance cruises. Since such cruises will probably take you farther across the water and keep you out longer, you will have that much more to take into account. Precautions include examining charts of the area where you intend to cruise and locating a variety of safe anchorages in case the weather turns nasty. It is also wise to take along extra clothes—a sweat shirt, long pants, and a jacket—kept dry in a plastic trash bag. The farther you plan to go, the more forethought and caution you must use.

Many of the modifications or additions you make for racing will also serve for cruising—namely, the compass, water-bottle mounts, and bailer. One change in particular can make your boat more suitable for cruising. Most recreational shells come with at least one inspection port; converting the port provided so that it accepts a nylon sock-like insert will be useful. The insert will let you keep items, such as your wallet and lunch, safe and dry.

If you've decided that cruising suits you, you may never need to change boats. As stated earlier, most recreational boats make ideal day cruisers. On the other hand, cruising might become so interesting to you that you decide you want to take longer trips.

The length of your proposed journeys will be determined by three factors: your ability, your level of preparation, and the suitability of your boat. Long-distance rowing cruises are feasible, and they take place all the time. On the West Coast, people regularly row the 30 miles to Catalina Island, spend a day or two, and row back. The 60-mile journey from Newport Beach to San Diego is also popular with long-distance rowers. Each year more and more rowers are attracted to the Sea of Cortez, where they can row past the desert shore. In the Pacific Northwest, rowers take vacations to cruise the San Juan Islands, and each summer, someone takes the inland passage to Alaska. In the South, the Gulf of Mexico and Florida's inland waterway have become rowers' territory. Farther north on the Atlantic Coast, the Chesapeake Bay and the Delaware and Potomac rivers attract touring scullers. The Connecticut shore of Long Island Sound is a cruiser's paradise, with innumerable coves and rivers to explore. In late spring and summer, rowers take to the open ocean to explore the coasts of Massachusetts and Maine. In Germany, *Vanderruden* (literally, "wander rowing") is attracting hundreds of enthusiasts to lakes and rivers. Long-distance cruising offers some of the best rowing there is.

Just as racing requires new skills, so does cruising. Instead of power and speed, cruising requires planning, logistics, and endurance. The three factors of success—your ability, preparation, and the suitability of your boat—rank nearly equal in importance. You have to be prepared and know your limitations. Your planning and logistics cannot be haphazard; you must take every conceivable aspect of your journey into consideration. If you are well prepared, your boat is probably the least important element of the cruise. That is not to say you should try to row from Vancouver to Alaska in a leaky Sabot converted to oar power. Your boat must be sound and chosen with the conditions you expect to encounter in mind, but it doesn't have to be the newest and "best." Simple preparedness will allow you to overcome greater obstacles than you could surmount with the "best" boat and inadequate preparations.

Preparation for your cruise can and should be one of the most enjoyable aspects of the entire project. Before a cruise, the list of things to do may seem endless—buy charts, review cruising guides, procure a copy of the local tide tables, tear down and rebuild oarlocks, find a spare bulb for the flashlight, etc.—but what a delightful excuse to ignore more mundane chores like mowing the lawn. Anticipation of the voyage will be heightened as you make your plans and preparations. Time spent poring over charts, foreseeing contingencies, and working out ways around them will allow you to make your cruise confidently and safely. Making lists of everything you need, paring them down, and double-checking will pay off even before you push off from the beach. It will teach you a lot, not just about your voyage, but about you. Talking to others who know your proposed cruising grounds can be fascinating and educational, and what sculler doesn't love talking about rowing with another rower?

While you're preparing yourself and gathering your supplies, don't forget about the boat. Before a cruise is the time to do all the little jobs that you might have been putting off or ignoring. The squeaking seat that's easy to overlook during your daily row will become a major annoyance on a long cruise and could be an early warning signal of a more serious problem. Like every other problem or suspected problem, it should be dealt with before your departure.

As a cruiser, your idea of a "better" boat will be very different from a racer's. Cruisers need load-carrying capacity and seaworthiness more than they need raw speed, and they tend to favor shorter, sturdier, beamier boats with the lines of the early workboats: dories, peapods, and Whitehalls. Built from modern materials and fitted with sliding seats, these copies of traditional craft are great cruisers. With their greater beam, they can easily carry the weight of a cruiser's food, water, and camping gear. Though not nearly as fast as a recreational shell, a good traditional replica is far more seaworthy. While the recreational racer may be looking at an ARS, Vancouver 21, or California Wherry as his "better" boat, the cruiser will work his way back to the left and farther up Gordie Nash's chart to find the Appledore Pod or New York Whitehall.

You don't need to race a shell over a 2,000-meter course, race a recreational shell across 30 miles of open ocean, or cruise 200 miles to grow as a sculler. Every time you take your boat out, you can be improving. You can get the most out of each workout by making each catch, stroke, release, and recovery as perfect as you possibly can. Feeling yourself become more efficient in and aware of your motion over the water is a better indicator of progress than simply buying another boat. Each time you row, go farther or faster or make a cleaner stroke than the time before. You will improve as long as you work at it, and that is real growth.

What It's Like Out There

Instructional books tend to be dry, almost by definition. It's difficult, for example, to convey the pleasure of rowing in a discussion of the proper ratio of recovery to stroke or the effect of positive oarlock pitch. The three essays that follow have been written in the hope that they will give you a feel for what it's like to be aboard a recreational boat. They will also give you a chance to meet some of the people who make recreational rowing the friendly, supportive sport it is. The first of these essays is the story of a rowing seminar hosted by the Sausalito Rowing Club; the second is an account of a recreational boat race staged on Lake Tahoe; and the third is my account of a solo cruise to the Channel Islands off the California coast. These three pieces will illustrate three very different aspects of this multifaceted sport.

A ROWING SEMINAR

The Sausalito Rowing Club, located on Richardson's Bay on the north shore of San Francisco Bay, is one of the most active recreational rowing clubs in California. The club's orientation is almost exclusively recreational. The boats on the racks in the boathouse are sturdily built, designed for open-water rowing. Several members are well known for representing the club outside the Bay area. Aside from staging races and providing a fleet of club-owned recreational boats for its non-boat-owning members, the Sausalito Rowing Club does its members and the general public a great service by hosting a series of rowing seminars. During the winter months, these take the form of lectures given by experts in such fields as racing tactics and physical training. As soon as spring arrives, the workshops move outdoors and become hands-on rowing sessions.

In late April 1985, the Sausalito Rowing Club cosponsored one of its seminars with several recreational boat and equipment manufacturers—Rowing Crafters, Small Craft, Open Water Rowing, Christian Maas Boat Company, and Pacific Oars. The gathering took place in front of the rowing club at Schoonmaker Beach. Although the spring sun was warm, the air was chilled by a 12-to-15-knot westerly blowing cold air in from the Pacific. Offshore, the Bay was a swarm of large sail and power boats participating in the Pacific Intra-Club Yacht Association Opening Day ceremonies, an annual event in which Bay-area sailors celebrate the arrival of another boating season. Water conditions on Richardson's Bay varied from very smooth water nearshore to an 8-to-12-inch chop out at the wind line. Farther offshore the confused wakes of large yachts made for rougher conditions.

The hosting club and sponsors had assembled a diverse fleet of boats, many equipped with new sculls from Pacific Oars, for the participants to compare. Several people were on hand to give rowing instruction at both the beginner and intermediate levels. Gordie Nash of Rowing Crafters and Christian Maas of Christian Maas Boat Company not only brought boats, but stood ready to help tune any boats brought by seminar participants. Two discussion groups were scheduled for the afternoon, one on physical fitness and the second on the hull shape of recreational rowing boats. Anyone interested in rowing was sure to find something of interest in the course of the day.

The cold westerly cut into the attendance slightly, but nearly a hundred enthusiasts braved the chill wind to find boats lining the beach and builders and dealers eager to explain the advantages of each. A selection of stable boats, such as the Small Craft Warning, had been fitted with tether lines so that neophyte rowers could learn the fundamentals of sliding-seat rowing while safely leashed to their instructors. Although there were several entry-level boats, the seminar was geared toward the more advanced oarsman. Gordie Nash had brought his race-winning California Wherry and the new Rec-Racer from France. Bill Fisher of Small Craft, who was scheduled to participate in the hull-shape seminar, was on hand with the first ARS II to be seen in California. Christian Maas, the other member of the hull-shape seminar, had come with two boats—his popular, fast Vancouver 21 and his newest creation, the Aero. Between the entry-level boats and the advanced racers, there was a wide selection of recreational boats, including peopod designs for cruising or load-carrying, doubles and a triple for those who like to row with a partner, and singles of varying speeds and stability.

Clusters of participants formed, their sizes changing as people shifted from one group to another. Beginners, awed by the array of boats on the beach, tended to gather around the wet-suit-clad instructors. After listening carefully to instructions, they formed queues and waited patiently for their turn in a boat. They were, if a little nervous, anxious to take their first strokes in a sliding-seat boat. Meanwhile, more advanced rowers were watching as Gordie Nash tuned the rigging and pitched the oarlocks of a club member's boat. Small groups formed around each boat on the beach, examining and critiquing hull shape and rigging, and opening inspection ports to check out construction.

The Rec-Racer received rather cursory inspection, but the ARS II drew larger crowds that tended to stay longer. There was a lot to see on the new boat. The Sausalito Rowing Club owns one of the original ARS's, as do several of the members, so most of the seminar participants were familiar with the older design. The new hull shape, with far less rocker in both the bow and stern, came under careful scrutiny. Everyone agreed the boat would be potentially faster in smooth water, but her ability in rougher going, a strong point of the older design, was severely questioned. While the redesigned hull received its fair share of attention, the feature of the new boat that caused most comment was the wing. A Kevlar and carbon fiber wing, modeled after the rig used on several European racing shells, had been molded to replace the stainless steel riggers supporting the oarlocks. Shaped like a blunted V, the wing attaches to the deck aft of the foot stretchers, its apex pointing aft and its arms sweeping forward to hold the oarlocks. Black against the white hull, the wing quickly earned the ARS II the nickname "bat boat." One of the first people to row the new boat pronounced the new wing an engineering, though perhaps not an aesthetic, success. The wing is far stiffer than the old stainless rigging.

While some waited their turn with the ARS II, others drifted off to join a group of serious racers around Christian Maas. As his audience grew, Maas explained the differences that made his new Aero faster than his race-winning Vancouver 21. When Maas finished, there was a rush to be the first into the boat. While the winner launched, most of the others formed a waiting line. Some people drifted down the beach, planning to return when the demand slackened.

As the oarsmen moved up and down the beach from boat to boat, they talked rowing and scanned the water. At times, they paused to watch a boat row by, critiquing both the boat's and the oarsman's performance. The wooden sculls from Pacific Oars received as much attention as the boats. The new oars were compared favorably to the Paintedosis, practically the industry standard, and even the people who regularly rowed with Concept II carbon fiber oars were impressed.

A small group formed at Gordie Nash's California Wherry, many people drawn by the boat's impressive race record. Those who rowed the boat commented as much on her instrumentation as her seakindly hull. Nash had surrounded his stretchers with a series of digital instruments, including a speedometer, stroke meter, compass, and watches for time-from-start and real time. One of the first things an oarsman would tell the next one in line was how fast he had gotten the boat going; the digital speedo gave readings exact to a tenth of a knot.

As morning turned to afternoon, the breeze freshened but it still failed to cool the enthusiasm of the participants. Nearly every available boat was on the water constantly, and an eager group awaited each beaching. While a new oarsman took his place in sliding seat, the one who had just vacated the seat gave his evaluation to those still waiting their turn.

At one point in the early afternoon, Christian Maas expressed some concern over the long absence of a man who had taken out his Aero. Gordie Nash immediately launched his California Wherry to row downwind in search of the missing oarsman. As Gordie disappeared in the direction of San Francisco Bay proper and the multitude of power and sail boats participating in the Opening Day ceremonies, the object of his search reappeared from upwind. The "missing" oarsman turned in the Aero and joined a group waiting to take out the Vancouver 21. Half an hour later, Gordie returned after a brisk row. Pulling strongly at 22 strokes per minute, he drove the California Wherry through the chop created by the headwind, demonstrating the boat's seaworthiness. A glance at the beach told him the Aero had returned safely, and he smiled as he turned his boat over to a seminar participant. He had enjoyed a good row in the kind of conditions that favor his boat and style.

The cold wind finally took its toll. Everyone had rowed all the boats he had come to row. Inspection ports had been opened and boats peered into; oars had been compared; questions, asked and answered. Many people who had never experienced the thrill of sliding-seat rowing had been able to row one of the boats they had watched and wondered about. Perhaps most importantly, old friendships had been renewed at this first gathering of the season, and new ones had formed. Plans had been made for rendezvous at various races or cruises scheduled throughout the spring, summer, and fall. Whatever the level of the participants, they had all gathered a lot of information. Many people were wet and everyone was cold, so the discussion program planned for late afternoon was rescheduled for a later date. After boats and oars were put away, the seminar dissolved into smaller groups who fled the cold of Schoonmaker Beach for homes, restaurants, or bars where they could continue their discussions and compare their impressions of boats and oars.

THE ANNUAL NORTH TAHOE ROWING REGATTA

Most recreational races on the West Coast are held in the open ocean or on an arm of the sea, but once a year ocean rowers are treated to an exception. One of the most popular annual events in the West is the Lake Tahoe North End Rowing Club's North Tahoe Rowing Regatta. Most rowers block out that weekend on their calendars as soon as the date is set—the event is a "must." There are several reasons that the six-year-old event has the great draw it does. A lot of the credit goes to its organizer, Peter Thompson, who puts in untold hours of organizing and planning. Then, of course, Peter has an ideal venue. The combination of organization and location regularly brings people from as far away as Southern California, Puget Sound, and Boulder, Colorado. But the majority of entrants come from San Francisco and the Central California coast, the most active area for recreational rowing on the West Coast. No matter where they come from, ocean rowers love Lake Tahoe. There are no tides or currents to contend with, and clothes and bodies aren't encrusted with salt after a row. And there is the view.

Lake Tahoe is magnificent. Its surface is 6,200 feet above sea level, but it forms the floor of a valley surrounded by 10,000-foot peaks. The upper elevations hold snow usually well into July, wreathing the blue of the lake with white. No high-mountain puddle, Tahoe is 26 miles long and 10 to 12 miles wide. Over 1,600 feet deep, the lake contains enough water to flood the state of Texas to a depth of 14 inches.

North and east of San Francisco in the Sierra Nevada Range, Tahoe straddles the California-Nevada border. The lake offers the summer visitor intense sun, clear fresh water, and, on the Nevada side, gambling and all the other attractions of the big hotel-casinos. Many visiting rowers find the colors of the region startling. Southern Californians are used to seeing a lot of gray sky, caused by either smog or haze, and gray ocean. Most of the colors are muted. The palm and eucalyptus trees are not a real green, but more a drab gray-green. Even on the central coast and in San Francisco there is a lot of gray from the prevailing fog. But not in Tahoe! In the mountains, under a brilliant sun, the thin air is a beautiful, intense, cobalt blue, setting off the whiteness of a few thin clouds. The lake itself is spectacular—like water in the South Pacific, it changes from gin-clear at the shore through every imaginable shade of greenish blue to a pristine azure in the depths. The trees (real trees, not their Southern Californian cousins) are bright green and thick on the slopes, except where they have been cleared for ski runs. In the high elevations, snow as white as the clouds glistens in the bright sunshine.

Traditionally, the regatta is held in late June, one of the prettiest and most peaceful times on the lake. The weather is usually bright and clear, and the crowds are thin. The skiers are gone, and the summer visitors have yet to arrive in force. For the first five years of its existence, the regatta was staged at The Boatworks, a Tahoe City mall and marina. The location was beautiful, but parking and setup space were severely limited. As there was no beach or ramp, boats had to be lowered from a retaining wall into the water and retrieved the same way. The sixth annual running of the event was moved to Lake Forest Beach, a narrow sand and pebble beach backed by forest.

Lake Forest Beach is a popular swimming and boardsailing beach, with shallow waters and, a few hundred feet offshore, one of only two islands in the lake. (The little island has been described as "beautiful" by some and "a tumbleweed" by other, less poetically inclined observers.) Parking still remained a problem, but the beach provided plenty of setup area, and launching was as simple as pushing your boat into the water.

The first boats began to arrive three hours before the 0900 start, finding a pair of nude bathers who thought they had the beach to themselves. By the 0800 skippers' meeting, there were about 70 boats of varying sizes and designs on the beach. A few kayaks and canoes were there, but the overwhelming majority of entrants were rowers. They came in every boat imaginable—from fixed-seat dories and beautiful, bright-finish, lapstrake Whitehalls to a quad with (shorthand for a four-oarsmen shell with a coxswain) and several other pure racing shells. While both ends of the pulling-boat spectrum were well represented, most of the entries and the interest lay in the center of the design range. Lake Forest Beach was a virtual boat show of recreational rowing boats. Practically everything was there, from the Alden Single, the boat that started the whole trend, to the Aero, the latest expression of the boatbuilder's art. There were California Wherries, Small Craft Singles, Rec-Racers, Alden Trainers, a fleet of Vancouver 21s (the predecessor to the Aero), and a brace of the new ARS "winged wonders." Before the race, the various boats received cursory examinations, but most of the attention was directed at conditions on the lake and at two men.

Conditions couldn't have been better—the lake was mirror-smooth and there wasn't a breath of wind. The sun was bright, and the only question on most people's minds was what effect the altitude would have. Several who had rowed the day before reported headaches, shortness of breath, and other symptoms of altitude sickness. Those who had arrived from sea level just in time to launch their boats chose not to hear these comments. The two men who were attracting the attention of most of the competitors were Gordie Nash and Christian Maas. Both from the Bay area, they have been rivals in recreational rowing races for a long time. Gordie, owner of Rowing Crafters, made a name for himself with his own California Wherries and, more recently, as West Coast representative of Small Craft, rowing their ARS.

Christian, builder of the Vancouver 21 and Aero, has a long string of victories in his own boats.

Gordie had brought a new ARS rigged with wings, as opposed to the more traditional stainless steel rigging. His boat featured an array of electronic equipment clustered around the stretchers, including digital compass, knotmeter, log and stroke meter, along with real time and time-from-start watches. Christian brought the same Aero he had used to win the 10-mile Bay-to-Bay Race in San Diego the month before and several shorter races since. The Aero is a simpler design than the ARS and appears small and fragile beside it. Christian's accessories consisted of a sailboat compass and a water bottle.

While they speculated about the outcome of the race, which would probably come down to a battle between Gordie and Christian, the competitors went about their pre-race preparations. Some slathered sunscreen on the backs of their necks, the tops of their ears, and their upper thighs, the places rowers always get burned. Water bottles were filled and stashed so they would come easily to hand. Some of the boats received final tweaks as rowers changed their buttons or foot stretchers by fractions of an inch, and lubrication was applied to oar collars and seat axles. Both Gordie and Christian were interrupted in their own preparations by rowers seeking advice and help. Finally everyone was ready, and the boats shoved off from the beach.

With more than 70 starters, it was obvious the original plan of starting the boats between the island and the beach would not be feasible; there simply wasn't enough room to get the boats lined up. The alternate plan, to extend the starting line through the island, favored the outboard end of the line, and most of the starters congregated on the lake side of the island. Peter counted down the start, and, with a great flurry of oars, the race was underway.

The start went well, considering the number of boats on the line, but it took a little distance for the rowers to sort themselves out. Even with the extended line, there were at least two files of rowers, and some faster boats and oarsmen found themselves behind slower competitors at the countdown. Individual races began right after the start, as rowers of matching skill and speed sought each other out.

The course ran south-southwest, past Tahoe City, to a turning mark just off a restaurant in Sunny Side on the west shore. The first leg was 2.63 miles long, and the only trick, since there are no currents, was to miss Cedar Point, but not to row out too far, adding extra distance to the leg. The row was beautiful, the rowers were fresh, the water was clear and cool, and the sky was a brilliant blue. Passing Tahoe City, which is located on a small indentation, the shore was at a distance, but at Cedar Point the racers once again found themselves close to a thickly wooded shore, with only a few houses and condominiums breaking the line of trees. (At Tahoe even the condos are pretty.) They had the lake practically to themselves; only a few fishermen and water-skiers shared the water with them that early Saturday morning.

Brunch-goers on the outside deck at the restaurant at Sunny Side had a beautiful view of the competitors rounding the mark in front of them. The true racing shells seemed to take forever swinging around, while the more nimble recreational boats turned in little more than their own length. The fleet had fanned out on the leg down from Lake Forest Beach, and rowers who had not been within three boat lengths of another boat since shortly after the start found themselves rounding overlapped with three or four other boats.

Theoretically, the second leg of the course, 4.56 miles northeast to Dollar Point, would have placed the leaders well outside the back markers, who had yet to round. This is an important consideration, because the boats are closing at between 10 and 14 miles per hour and the competitors have their backs to each other. The fanning out of the competitors on the first leg, however, meant that the leaders did not have a clear field. To get clear water, many racers had made too much southing on the first leg and were far out in the lake. To avoid this oncoming horde of boats, some of the leaders chose to hug the shore, sneaking past Cedar Point before starting their easting. There were many near misses and a few collisions, but no one was hurt and boat damage was minimal.

In the smooth conditions, racing shells led the way. The quad with from San Francisco's Dolphin Rowing Club and several pairs with and doubles were showing the way to the rest of the fleet, but neither Christian nor Gordie were letting the racing boats get too far ahead of them. The altitude began to tell on the long leg up to Dollar Point, the adrenaline from the start wore off, and the race became a long endurance contest. Some who had started too fast flagged; others who had been more conservative on the first leg began to pick off the boats in front of them. Some stroke rates dropped, but the leaders kept churning away.

For the leaders, the third leg of the course, just under 2.5 miles from Dollar Point back to Lake Forest Beach, turned into a sprint. Surprisingly, a pair with came in seconds ahead of the quad with, but it was the battle for third that had everyone on the beach cheering. Gordie and Christian were approaching the line, rowing for all they were worth. As the crowd cheered and applauded, Gordie crossed the line six seconds ahead of his rival. Both men were so exhausted that they couldn't climb out of their boats as they drifted up to the beach.

The beach began to fill with boats as racers finished, and Peter's organizing committee went to light the barbecues, but most of the competitors weren't really through with the race. They stood knee-deep in the lake quaffing their water bottles and anything cool that was handed them while they analyzed the race. As their strength returned, competitors exchanged boats to sample what was available on the beach. Not surprisingly, in greatest demand were Gordie's ARS and Christian's Aero.

Finally, even the most dedicated rowers had had enough, and the crowd retired to the barbecue where food and cold drinks awaited. Prizes were given and drawings were held, but the real prize was the opportunity to compete with and meet other rowers. As soon as the drawings were over, people drifted back to the beach for one more short row before loading their boats and heading down the mountain, vowing to return next year.

ANATOMY OF A CRUISE

Cruising in a pulling boat is the ideal way to learn about your cruising grounds. You move slowly through the environment, disturbing nothing and savoring each passing boat length. Each of your daily rows can be a mini-cruise, as you carefully examine your local lake or harbor and see what changes have taken place overnight. As time goes by, you will see and feel the effects of the different seasons on your home waters. Your boat will make you part of them; each change will affect you more directly.

While a daily row can make an interesting short cruise, more and more people are taking their pulling boats farther afield. Many recreational rowers treat their craft as true cruising boats. Cruising may well be the ultimate rowing experience, far more satisfying than either training or racing, for it combines all the best aspects of rowing. Cruising allows the sculler to spend time alone in his boat—not just an hour or two, but whole days at a stretch—developing his skills. It requires logistical expertise and endurance. A cruise is far more than the three or four days you spend in the boat; it is the culmination of all the planning, preparation, and anticipation that went into it, and it is all the knowledge and satisfaction you draw from it.

Before I began to think about cruising, I had made some long-distance rows, but these had always been passages from point A to point B, more like self-imposed endurance tests than true cruises. I had always been intent upon reaching my destination, not on enjoying the passage. When I gave some thought to a real cruise in a pulling boat, I realized my options were rather limited. Southern California's geography does not encourage cruises in rowing boats. The harbors lie far apart, and there are few safe bays in which to anchor. Most of the islands are far from shore, and there are no interesting rivers to explore. To the Southern Californian contemplating a cruise, just about every other area of the country looks better than his own home waters. In Central California, there are Monterey and Carmel Bays with three harbors and several safe anchorages, along with gorgeous scenery and intriguing wildlife. San Franciscans can explore the great Sacramento River delta. Washingtonians have the San Juan Islands, Vancouver Island with its fjordlike bays and coves, and the inland passage to Alaska. On the Atlantic side of the country, the Maine Coast is a cruiser's heaven, with 2,500 miles of shoreline and 3,500 islands to explore. Boston's Harbor Islands could keep a cruiser happy for years. Farther south are the protected waters of the Connecticut shore and the fascinating Chesapeake. The South has the Intracoastal Waterway running all the way to Florida. Lake rowers can choose the stark beauty of desert lakes such as Powell or wooded mountain lakes like Quinault, but Southern Californians have miles of monotonous coastline unbroken by harbors. Some California rowers load up their boats and drive to the Sea of Cortez or Central California to make their cruises, but I wanted to stay reasonably close to home.

I contemplated a trip to Catalina, 32 miles from my local harbor, but the round-trip, open-ocean passage seemed more like another endurance test than a cruise. Also, I wanted to cruise in relative isolation; in early summer, Catalina is too crowded for my taste.

A plane trip to San Francisco to compete in a sculling race solved the problem of where to cruise. On a beautifully clear morning, the plane passed over the Santa Barbara Channel Islands, and it was as if they shouted up to me that this was the perfect cruising ground for a pulling boat. I had seen the islands from the same flight dozens of times before, and I had raced yachts around them for years, but suddenly I was seeing them in a new way. I spent the rest of the flight categorizing everything I already knew about the islands and starting to plan the cruise.

The four islands that make up the group known as the Santa Barbara Channel Islands (or, more familiarly, the Channel Islands) are Anacapa, Santa Cruz, Santa Rosa, and San Miguel. The islands lie east to west in a string of convenient stepping stones. The closest to shore is Anacapa, just 11 miles from the entrance of Channel Islands Harbor at Oxnard. An 11-mile row was far more inviting than a 32-mile journey. Then there was the fact that the Channel Islands do not attract the hordes Catalina does. The islands are also reasonably close to my home, Oxnard being only a two-hour drive north.

Planning for the cruise started in earnest six weeks before the intended departure date, though quite a bit of thought had gone into it before that. I had drawn up long lists of equipment and provisions to buy and things to attend to. The first two items on my "to buy" list were an up-to-date cruising guide and a chart. Once those were purchased, planning went into high gear.

In recent years there have been some governmental changes affecting the Channel Islands, and they now fall under several different jurisdictions. They are both a national sanctuary and a national park, administered by a sanctuary manager and the National Park Service. Certain areas within the boundaries of the park are private property (such as Santa Cruz Island) and are patrolled by the Santa Barbara County Sheriff's Department, with landing permits issued on the mainland by the owners of the property. Once I had decided where I wanted to go, I set about learning what regulations and red tape would have to be dealt with. Fortunately, this was easily handled, and I could proceed with the more interesting job of planning what would be needed and exactly how the trip would be made.

If planning and preparedness are essential to the safety of your daily row, they are even more crucial to the safe and enjoyable completion of an extended cruise. The longer you are in the boat and the farther you go, the more planning you must do for the voyage. The trip was scheduled to last just three days, but I would have to be totally self-sufficient for the entire time. Nothing is available on these wild islands; anything you want or need you have to take with you— every drop of water, every crumb of food.

The boat I planned to use is ideal for this type of cruise. *Kavienga* (the name comes from the star paths followed by Polynesian navigators) is a much modified Appledore Pod. The hull is a standard fiberglass Appledore as supplied by Martin Marine. The design is a faithful reproduction of a New England peapod, proven by well over a hundred years of use on that rough coast. *Kavienga* is 16 feet long with a 37-inch beam. The Martin design is modified only in the interior, where a flat deck is laid over the stringers, and the Oarmaster has been replaced with a smaller, lighter, and stiffer custom-built rowing system. Her aluminum riggers give a pin-to-pin dimension of 61 inches. Flotation compartments are located fore and aft, and they have slightly more volume than the factory chambers. *Kavienga* is rigged to set a 55-square-foot spritsail, but for this voyage I chose to leave the sailing rig in the boathouse; this cruise was to be made under oar power alone.

After the cruising guide and chart, the next articles on my list were all safety items. I owned almost everything listed, but each needed to be carefully examined and tested to see that it functioned properly. The list of things to buy grew as each piece of equipment was tested. Spare bulbs for the flashlight, extra batteries for the flashlight and the lantern, and the first-aid kit needed to be restocked. Once all the safety equipment was selected and checked, it needed to be stored on the boat in such a way as to be instantly available. The PFD, with a whistle, strobe, and knife attached to it, was lashed to the mast partner, where nothing could block my access to it. My own favorite survival gear, a full wet suit and pair of swim fins, was stored aft, atop the stern flotation compartment.

One safety consideration on which I vacillated for some time was the number of oars to carry. Prudence called for two pairs; on the other hand, storage considerations and experience suggested that one spare oar would be enough. Storing two pairs of sculls aboard at night would consume quite a bit of space, and in more than 25 years of rowing, I had broken only two oars, about eight years apart. There was nothing to suggest I would break both oars on this cruise, so I decided to carry only a single spare.

Once the items on the safety list had been attended to, it was time to turn to the lists of boat-handling gear, provisions, and personal equipment. Each item on each list underwent three separate readings to weed out anything that was superfluous. After all, any gear I took that was not essential would mean just that much more weight to pull around, and it would also rob me of precious room in the boat. Once I had gathered everything together, I made a final check to make sure that all of it was really needed. The final heap of gear and provisions was quite large, and *Kavienga* seemed rather small.

It took several tries to store everything aboard with the proper fore-and-aft and port-to-starboard weight distribution and to make sure the items I would use the most were readily available. The large flotation compartments, each equipped with an inspection port, made tempting storage places, but I fought the urge for two reasons. The first was safety—anything stored in the compartments would displace air needed for flotation. The second was performance—*Kavienga*, like any other boat, handles better if her weight is centered, and keeping the flotation compartments empty would keep weight out of the ends.

Once the loading was completed, I did a rowing test with *Kavienga* fully laden. She felt slightly sluggish, but this wasn't going to be a race. She balanced well after a few minor adjustments to her trim, and we were ready to go. All that was left to do was to make and file a float plan and check the long-term weather forecast.

As I rounded the southern end of Channel Islands Harbor's detached breakwater, *Kavienga*'s bow rose sluggishly to the first ocean swell. The little peapod was heavily laden and she felt it. Though the cruise was planned for three days, she was carrying provisions to last for five in case the winds came up while I was on the islands. The prevailing northwesterlies didn't bother me; they always subside at night, allowing plenty of time to row to the mainland before they begin to build again. It was the wrong time of the year for the vicious southwesterlies, which bring rain in the winter months. What disturbed me was the possibility of Santa Anas. Blowing from the northeast, Santa Anas are strong winds off the inland desert that regularly reach speeds of 35 knots (winds of 60 to 80 knots are not unknown). Anacapa, my principal destination, is called "suicidal in Santa Ana conditions" by my cruising guide. Chances of a Santa Ana blow were slim according to the long-distance weather forecast, but having the food needed to weather a couple of extra days at anchor made me feel more secure.

Typically, on the morning I set out for Anacapa, the Santa Barbara Channel was socked in with what weathermen call "low clouds and haze" but Southern Californians know as "June gloom." It was dark and damp without even a slight lightening of the eastern horizon to foretell the coming dawn. About two dozen strokes away from the breakwater, I swung *Kavienga* around so that I faced my destination. All I could see was gray darkness. Anacapa Light, one of the most powerful lighthouses on the California coast, which is visible for 23 miles in clear weather, was not strong enough to penetrate the gloom. The oil islands that dot the channel were also hidden by the haze. I turned *Kavienga* around, took a compass reading, and began the 11-mile row to Anacapa's east end.

After about an hour of rowing, the eastern sky was beginning to lighten, and I decided it was time for a short break. A light had appeared faintly through the fog over my left shoulder. I used the hand-bearing compass to get a bearing on it and then sipped some water from the water bottle and ate a banana. After breakfast, I took a second bearing on the light. It hadn't gotten brighter, meaning that it was no closer, and the bearing hadn't changed, meaning that it was one of the offshore drilling platforms. In the Santa Barbara Channel, it is important to know what each light means. To get to the islands, you pass through a traffic lane, and it's vital to know whether a light is coming from a ship or an oil island. Anacapa Light was now piercing the haze, and a bearing off the light showed I'd been making a little southing, so I put some north into the course and went back to the oars.

Dawn was not beautiful that morning; it merely brought a lightening to the all-encompassing grayness. Glances over my shoulder showed the lump of Anacapa taking shape in the haze, and I went into my second hour of rowing. Finally, I took one last strong stroke with the starboard oar, and *Kavienga* swung her stern around, giving me a full view of my destination.

I was about half a mile off Anacapa's east end. The 80-foot Arch Rock with its 50-foot-high arch, considered the symbol of Anacapa and the Channel Islands, was tempting, but I didn't want to get too close to the rocks. Behind it, on the island proper, the light blinked 277 feet above me, and I could see the tile-roofed building that houses the park rangers. The haze softened the contours of the rugged island; 930-foot-high Vela Peak at the west end appeared just an indistinct mass.

Anacapa is 4½ miles long and not much more than a half-mile wide. It is, in fact, three islands, separated by narrow, impassable channels. Most of the island is very steep and uninviting. For all the tales of high winds and treacherous surf, the island was becalmed that morning. The westerly swell barely raised the thick kelp beds that protect the shore, hardly a cat's-paw of wind disturbed the glassy gray sea.

After celebrating an uneventful passage from the mainland with a small bag of trail mix and a long hit on the water bottle, it was time to move on. I slowly rowed along the north shore, past the lighthouse landing, where supplies for the rangers are lifted by crane. The cruising guide describes landing there as rather tricky—you must climb a metal ladder to reach the landing, and since there is no safe place to tie your dinghy, it must be lifted after you. Since *Kavienga* was my dinghy and there was no way she could be lifted, we proceeded along the coast toward Cathedral Cove, another half-mile away.

A pair of yearling seals met me near Cathedral Cove, but apparently I wasn't interesting enough to hold their attention, for after giving me a quick once-over, they dove and were gone. Cathedral Cove is more an indentation than a cove, but a well-placed spire of rock provides some protection from the prevailing winds. When I pulled in, there were already three boats sharing this sheltered spot. All were well offshore, kept away from the steep cliffs by thick kelp beds. Two of the boats, a Cal 25 and a Columbia 30, were rafted together, and the third, a Grand Banks trawler, was a few boat lengths away. Both sailing yachts, flying matching burgees, appeared deserted, but a heavyset man was sitting on the fantail of the Grand Banks enjoying his morning cup of coffee. He waved and I swung *Kavienga* toward his stern.

As I closed on the Grand Banks, the man hoisted himself out of his director's chair, took a long swallow of coffee and an equally long drag on his cigarette, then took the two steps to his brightly varnished rail and looked down at me. "Mornin'," he greeted me. Then, surveying the anchorage, he asked, "Where's your boat?"

"Morning," I responded, "I'm in it."

There followed several questions about my trip to the island, my proposed return to the mainland, and the state of my sanity. Finally he told me he was heading back to the mainland at noon "before it kicked up" and would be happy to give me a tow. I thanked him but declined the offer and moved off, looking for an anchorage. After a few moments, I pulled out of Cathedral Cove and rounded the spire to an anchorage on the west side of the rock. The cruising guide described this as a "temporary anchorage" due to its openness, but in the baylike conditions that day it was safe enough.

The water was clear, and I dropped the hook in 20 feet of water and backed down to set it, then let go the oars, and took a long look at my surroundings. With the hook down, I felt I had really arrived. It was still gray and overcast, conditions that would persist the entire cruise. I drained the water bottle, then carefully decanted water from one of the gallon jugs into the smaller bottle. My theory was that if I slipped while taking a drink, I would risk losing only the small amount of water in the hand bottle, not a whole gallon. Then I moved the rowing station into the bow and stretched out on the deck to read.

Something bumped *Kavienga*'s hull, and I sat bolt upright. I had dozed off. I found myself eyeball to eyeball with four yuppie types. All four, two men and two women, wore bright blue T-shirts emblazoned with the same burgee I had seen on the two sailing boats at Cathedral Cove. They were all smiling at me from a yellow inflatable, and holding *Kavienga*'s gunwale with four pairs of hands. All the fingernails were neatly trimmed and cleaned, and the women's were freshly painted.

"Hi," they chorused. Then their leader announced, "Man on the Grand Banks at Cathedral said some nut rowed over here from the mainland. Did you?"

I assured them that I was the nut. One of the women told me they had rowed to the lighthouse landing, then all the way back to their boats, and over to me. Looking at their inflatable and its stubby little oars, I was impressed. They invited me aboard their sailboats for "bloodies," and when I declined, they offered to take me back to Ventura with them. There seemed to be some conspiracy afoot to tow me away from the island after all my hard work to get there. We chatted some more. They declared it was time for "bloodies" and were off.

By the time my visitors left, it was nearly noon, so I had a small drink of water and an orange, then re-rigged *Kavienga*, hoisted the anchor, and set out for Frenchy's, where I planned to anchor for the night. A straight-line course from Cathedral Cove to Frenchy's, almost two miles away, took me well offshore the central part of Anacapa. Some of the kelp is so thick, especially at the east end of the central island, that it extends over a quarter-mile offshore. Several seals were working this area. Contending with them were two men on a Skipjack.

We waved, but there were no comments about my sanity, for which I was grateful. I had a delightful row over smooth water, watching the island and its fringing kelp move slowly past.

Frenchy's, the most sheltered anchorage on Anacapa, is named for a French hermit who lived there for some 30 years. The anchorage is just west of the passage between the west and central islands. It is not quite as pretty as Cathedral Cove, but there were no boats in the area, which made it quite attractive to me. Before putting down the hook, I turned toward the small sand and rock beach and made my way through the thick kelp beds. I had been aboard for quite a while and wanted to stretch my legs.

The sea was still calm and beaching was easy. With the aid of an inflatable bumper used as a roller, *Kavienga* was easy to pull out of the water. Most of western Anacapa is closed to the public because it is the primary rookery for the California brown pelican, but the east end is open and is a popular landing. To stretch my legs, I took the easy hike across the island to where some tide pools are located. The westerly began to fill in at a pleasant 10 to 12 knots. On my way back, I saw the two sailboats from Cathedral Cove offshore. Their mainsail covers were tightly in place as they motored northwest toward Santa Cruz. The Skipjack that had been fishing the kelp beds had anchored off Frenchy's, but there was no sign of those aboard. I hoped they would be quiet neighbors.

I dined on the beach, setting my Coleman stove in *Kavienga*'s lee and fixing a pot of noodles, chicken, and mushrooms, followed by a cup of tea. After cleaning up, I put *Kavienga* back in the water and rowed out to a spot in the anchorage some distance from the skipjack. I dropped the hook In 25 feet of water and backed down, digging it into the sand and small rocks that formed the bottom. To make as much room as possible in *Kavienga*, the sculls were left in their locks, but I brought the blades aboard and tucked them under the mast partner. I stood the spare oar upright, its handle passing through the mast partner and resting in the mast base. The sliding seat was lifted out of its mounting holes and placed across the stern. The result was a wide, uncluttered deck. After positioning the inflatable mattress and sleeping bag, I lay down to read. The book didn't hold my interest; instead I thought of the day. I had come 14 miles, no farther than many of my daily rows, and far shorter than many recreational races, but I had entered another world. Here I was lying at anchor off an uninhabited island. The fishermen on the Skipjack were quiet, and I could almost imagine that I was totally alone in the world. Before I fell asleep, I lashed the battery-powered lantern to the vertical oar, setting my anchor light 9 feet above the waterline.

I awoke to a noisy, foggy morning. The noise didn't bother me at all; it was caused by crying gulls and barking seals, not motors or radios. *Kavienga* was quickly put in order and rowed back to the beach, where I breakfasted on a cup of tea, dry cereal, and an orange, and then did some stretches in preparation for the day's row. I had expected to be a little stiff from the previous day's row and sleeping on the boat, but to my surprise, I felt great.

As I rowed out of Frenchy's, the two fishermen on the Skipjack paused in the preparation of their rigs to wave. I returned the wave—they had been perfect neighbors. There is a large cave just west of Frenchy's that can be explored by dinghy, but I didn't want to take *Kavienga* in with her long sculls. On that hazy morning, West Anacapa seemed alive with seals—they were three and four deep on the rocks west of the cave, and sleek heads would frequently break the surface just outside the thick kelp beds. One gave me a start by surfacing in the blind spot behind my left shoulder and exhaling loudly. A few gulls dove on me, but when they discovered I had no bait to offer them, they went back to the sea.

Santa Cruz Channel, separating Santa Cruz and Anacapa, is only 5 miles wide, and on this morning it was flat calm. San Pedro Point, Santa Cruz's east end, lies slightly northwest of Anacapa's western end. My intention was to explore part of the north shore, so I headed away from Anacapa before I got to the east end.

Halfway across the channel, I was just thinking the passage was too easy, when a long line of white water off my starboard side caught my eye. I stopped rowing to concentrate on this possible threat. My first thought was that it was the wake of a powerboat, but I hadn't heard any engine noise. There was nothing there. The gray water was flat and unbroken. Suddenly, the water broke again—it was a school of dolphin. Traveling in a line abreast, at least a hundred animals were moving at flank speed. They broke the surface in unison, then dove, leaving a white line of disturbed water a quarter-mile long. I rested on my oar handles and watched. They weren't feeding. They were on their way somewhere in a hurry. Once more they rose to the surface, then they passed under me as if I weren't there, and I swiveled in my seat to watch until the haze swallowed them up. They had silently reminded me that I was in alien territory, an intruder in a fragile craft.

A miscalculation on the part of any one of those animals could have capsized or sunk *Kavienga*, leaving me treading water in the middle of the channel. I put a little more effort into the oars and headed toward Santa Cruz.

A pair of guano-covered rocks lying offshore are the landmark for Scorpion and Little Scorpion anchorages. As I closed on the island, I could see nine yachts anchored at Little Scorpion. The Cal and Columbia were again rafted together—the four yuppies were there ahead of me. I approached with the rough shore on the port side, heading into the bay of Little Scorpion. It was just 0900; people were moving about on the moored boats, a single dinghy was heading into the beach, and another was approaching the guano-covered rocks. One of the yuppies spotted me and they all called and waved. When I waved back, I could hear them explain to someone on a neighboring yacht that I was the nut they had been talking about. One of the men held up a jug of "bloodies," but I chose not to notice him. I crossed paths and exchanged nods with the man taking the dinghy to the beach, then continued on, swinging past the beach and back out beside the rocks. There is a shallow rock spine connecting the rocks to the shore, so I decided to use caution and round the rocks to Scorpion. The rocks are honeycombed with caves, and it would have been interesting to explore them, but *Kavienga*'s long sculls made that impossible. More caves dot the cliff between Little Scorpion and Scorpion, and the second inflatable was just disappearing into one as I passed.

The larger of the two Scorpion anchorages is by far the less popular. Scorpion is not as protected and features poor holding ground. I had the bay to myself, except for a pair of seals feeding near the dilapidated pier that serves the ranch. I put *Kavienga* on the beach and had a long drink of water and a bag of trail mix. It was pleasant there. The two seals continued to feed near the old pier, and gulls and pelicans dove into the water offshore. I took a short walk, then lay in the sand to read. I had been on the beach for about an hour when a faint eddy of the westerly began to bring the smell of guano from the offshore rocks. I could imagine what it would be like on a hot day. It was enough to make me launch and head out of the bay. It was time to start back for Anacapa anyway. Just because the westerlies had not filled in strongly the previous afternoon didn't mean they wouldn't come with a vengeance that day, and I didn't want to be caught out between the two islands if it began to blow.

As it turned out, I had delayed my departure almost too long. It was blowing a gentle 5 to 7 knots when I left Scorpion. In the half-hour it took me to reach San Pedro Point, the breeze had filled in to a good 10 knots. The water of the channel was riffled, Anacapa waited in the haze. The mainland was obscured, and it dawned on me I hadn't seen it since I had passed the halfway point on the row over to Anacapa.

Normally, rough wind and sea conditions don't faze me when I row. In fact, I enjoy pushing a boat into a headwind, then turning and riding the wind and chop back home, but I wasn't in my home waters. Ten knots of wind was hardly a problem, but there was no reason to think it was not going to keep building. I was alone off an unfriendly shore. There were two choices. I could go for Anacapa or swing around San Pedro Point and go into the wide roadstead at Smuggler's Cove to wait and see what happened. If the wind did build, preventing a passage to Anacapa that afternoon, it would mean the trip back to the mainland the following morning would be a long one, over 20 miles.

I looked to the north and didn't see any whitecaps. I put a lot of power into that first catch. The first whitecaps appeared when I was just a quarter-mile off the point. I let the oars drop and took the time to shift the anchor from just abaft the forward flotation tank to just forward of the rear tank. Moving 20 pounds of ballast 11 feet aft changed *Kavienga*'s trim significantly. In the course of the cruise, she had begun to take on a slight bow-down trim because the provisions I had consumed had been stored aft. Shifting the anchor brought her bow up. This would give me an extra margin of safety if the seas built, making her far less likely to bury her bow.

The westerly filled rapidly, pushing through the teens to the low twenties. The seas built with the wind until I was looking at more whitecaps than unbroken sea. Spray blew across *Kavienga* regularly. The 6-foot swells came hissing up from astern, lifted *Kavienga*'s heavy stern, and pushed her along until they sped past; then she wallowed in the trough until the next one gave her a lift. I shortened my stroke and concentrated on keeping the blades high on recovery. The wind and waves were giving me added forward speed. I was pulling just enough to keep from broaching and generate a little extra speed to climb each overtaking wave. To catch a wave, I would add some power to my stroke and then, after the release, hold the layback position to keep my weight forward. Once on the wave, I would quickly slide through the recovery, exaggerating the height of the blades, and hold the catch position to keep more weight aft so the bow would lift.

My destination was East Fish Camp on the southern shore of Anacapa, a relatively secure anchorage in a westerly. There was no great foresight in this planning, I had just wanted to return via the south shore rather than the north, which I had already visited. As I swept around Anacapa's west end into the lee of towering Vela Peak, the swells curled around the end of the island and gave me a great ride down the southern shore until they petered out. If *Kavienga* had been lighter, the ride would have been better, but even heavily laden, she moved beautifully on the swells.

Normally I would have gone in to explore the coast and take a second look at the tide pools I had explored the day before, but I was wet and tired, and East Fish Camp was still two miles away, so I passed them by. Thick kelp guards the south side of Anacapa, and I kept well offshore. Between Middle and West Anacapa I was hit again by the full force of the westerly, but this time I was taking it on the beam. Before I could get into the lee of the middle island, I had been blown nearly a hundred yards southeast. If the wind blew tomorrow while I was making the passage to the mainland, it would be a real problem.

East Fish Camp, a commercial fisherman's anchorage, was a welcome sight. The kelp-choked water was smooth and calm, the steep island protecting it from the westerlies. I pulled through the thick kelp, startled as a seal surfaced just off my stern, and anchored close to the nearly vertical shore in about 20 feet of water. I drained the water bottle, took off my soaked T-shirt, and moved the rowing rig so I could lie down. In retrospect, it had been a challenging, exciting passage.

As the afternoon wore on, it appeared I would have East Fish Camp all to myself that night. I hadn't seen another boat since leaving the Scorpion anchorages. I boiled a can of tomato soup and drank it while preparing chicken and noodles in my single pan. Dinner was topped off with a pot of tea, and *Kavienga* was set up for the night.

It was cold and damp when I awoke. A true fog, not the typical haze, had set in during the night, and visibility had closed right down. I had a cup of tea and a can of soup to ward off the chill and waited for sunrise. The sun didn't help the visibility or the temperature. After sunrise, I could see 200 to 300 yards through the damp grayness. Rowing in fog is better than being caught offshore in 20 knots of wind blowing perpendicular to your course, so up came the anchor. I left the spare scull up with the lantern turned on. It wasn't much, but some sharp-eyed skipper might see it in the fog. Before starting across the channel, I removed the whistle from the PFD and hung it around my neck, and then took the time to restow *Kavienga*'s gear. The anchor went aft again, but a couple of small items moved forward, giving her just a slight bow-up trim. I had stalled long enough; the blades went into the water, and I gave my first easy stroke.

I went east, close to the fringing kelp bed and directly under the light and bleating foghorn, until I came to the arch rock. There was absolutely no wind, but I suspected a slight southerly current, so I decided to steer on the thin side of the 022-degree course back to the mainland. This would also compensate for any westerly that filled in while I was rowing. The fog was sure to dissipate before I reached the mainland, and I would be able to update my navigation then.

Anacapa Light was lost in the fog after very few strokes, but her mournful foghorn kept me company every 15 seconds. Between bleats of the foghorn, I listened for any other sounds in the fog. If there was anyone else sharing the water with me, I had to be aware of him; he certainly wasn't going to see me.

After about an hour, I relaxed somewhat. The fog hadn't lifted—in fact, it seemed to have closed in a bit more—but I should have been through the traffic lane by that time. To make sure, I put in another 15 minutes before stopping. My break consisted of a long drink of water and a banana while I watched the trailing sculls for any sign of a current. The water seemed as still as the air, and I decided to steer an honest 022-degree course, reasoning that I was already high of the breakwater. If the fog didn't lift to allow me to update my navigation, I was going to bump into the coast before I could see it. The beach north of the detached breakwater is sandy, and there didn't seem to be a ground swell running, so that was reassuring. Then there were the foghorns and lights on the breakwater. Surely I wasn't going to hit that.

I had just taken up the oars again when I heard the faint rumblings of a motor. The fog was playing tricks with the sound; first it came from the mainland, then from directly astern. The only thing the fog didn't mask was that the sound was getting louder, coming nearer. It would have been foolish to row, I might move right into its path. As the sound increased, I could tell it wasn't a freighter or tanker, but a small boat—small, but surely big enough to sink *Kavienga* if it rammed her. The noise was increasing at an alarming rate—whoever it was was making good time through the thick fog. I finally decided the boat was outward bound from Channel Islands Harbor toward the islands. It was close enough that I could not mistake the direction. I only hoped it was steering 202 degrees for Anacapa's east end, not heading on a more northerly course for the west end or any of the Santa Cruz anchorages. I dipped my starboard oar and swung to the north, then dug in with both oars.

I never saw the boat, but I felt its wake as it lifted *Kavienga*'s stern. Shaken, I paused for a few minutes before turning back on my course. The operator of that vessel was obviously unaware that I was on the water and, considering the limited visibility, would have run me down long before he could have altered course.

The fog never really lifted, but it thinned so that there was a half-mile of visibility when I spotted the light at the northern end of the breakwater. I was about a hundred yards north of my dead reckoning landfall, just about twice the distance I rowed taking evasive action. I congratulated myself on a reasonably accurate landfall and patted *Kavienga*'s hull. She had performed well and done everything that was asked of her. All that remained was to get her out of the water, shower and shave, and start planning the next cruise.

Appendix 1   Nutrition
by
Patricia A. Ingram, M.S., R.D.

FOOD AS FUEL

Food provides the fuel necessary for carrying on the body's basic functions. Athletes need to eat especially well in order to perform to the best of their abilities. Diet affects size, strength, and endurance. The components of a well-balanced diet are carbohydrates, proteins, fats, vitamins, minerals, and water.

Carbohydrates

Carbohydrates are the main source of quick energy. They are stored in the blood as glucose and in the liver and muscle tissue as glycogen. Glucose is the form from which energy is derived. When the blood's supply of glucose is depleted, stored glycogen converts to glucose to maintain energy levels. Therefore, glycogen is particularly important in endurance events such as long-distance rowing.

Carbohydrates include simple sugars such as table sugar, brown sugar, molasses, and honey, which are digested rapidly, and complex sugars, or starches, such as rice, pasta, grains, and beans. About 50 percent of one's daily calories should come from carbohydrates. Athletes may want to consume even more a few days before an endurance event. Most of the carbohydrates consumed should be complex carbohydrates. Carbohydrates provide 4 calories per gram of food.

Protein

Protein builds and repairs body tissues. The common belief that eating extra protein will increase muscle mass is not true. The daily protein requirement does not increase with exercise. Protein is not an efficient source of energy and therefore will not help the athlete who consumes more than is needed. In fact, excessive amounts of protein may be harmful. Good sources of protein include meat, poultry, fish, eggs, milk and dairy products, nuts, and legumes. About 15 to 20 percent of one's daily calories should come from protein. Proteins, like carbohydrates, provide 4 calories per gram of food.

Fat

Fat functions as a carrier of fat-soluble vitamins and provides essential fatty acids. Stored fat is good insulation from the cold. Fats, like carbohydrates, are an important source of energy during endurance events. However, they are not a source of quick energy. Food sources of fat include butter, margarine, oils, and salad dressings. About 25 to 30 percent of one's daily calories should come from fat. Fats are the most concentrated source of energy, providing 9 calories per gram of food, compared to carbohydrates and proteins, which provide 4 calories per gram.

Vitamins and Minerals

Vitamins and minerals are necessary for the body's chemical reactions. Exercise does not increase the requirement for these nutrients. Vitamin and mineral supplements are usually unnecessary. Eating a well-balanced diet is the best way to meet the need for vitamins and minerals.

A common belief has it that salt tablets are necessary to replace the sodium lost in sweat. However, sodium can be easily replaced by eating a well-balanced diet. Salt tablets may actually be dangerous because of their dehydrating effect.

Fluid

Water is essential to life and all body processes. The average requirement is approximately two quarts of water a day. With exercise, the need for water increases, and hot weather increases it even more. Before an endurance event, you should drink several cups of water. During the event, you should drink several times per hour. When fluid intake is too low, energy levels decrease more rapidly.

Commercial electrolyte drinks are not recommended, because they tend to be high in sodium and sugar, both of which can be dehydrating.

PRE-COMPETITION MEAL

What you eat before an event of short duration will not affect your performance much. However, over-eating just before an event may cause some gastro-intestinal discomfort.

The pre-competition meal should be eaten at least three hours ahead so that food can be properly digested. The amount of protein and fat should be kept to a minimum because these nutrients take longer to digest. Also, foods high in sugar are not recommended; they can dehydrate you or lower your blood sugar, causing poor performance.

It is important to remember that no pre-competition meal or food will, in itself, guarantee good results. You must consume a well-balanced diet regularly and train properly for your event in order to perform well.

The basic food groups are recommended to achieve and maintain good nutrition. They are listed below:

Milk/Dairy Group
Milk, cheese, yogurt, ice cream, pudding.

Children – 3 or more servings per day
Teenagers – 4 or more servings
Adults – 2 or more servings

Meat/Meat Substitute Group
Beef, veal, pork, lamb, poultry, fish, eggs, dried beans or peas, nuts.
2 or more servings

Fruit/Vegetable Group
Include at least one dark-green or deep-yellow vegetable and at least one fruit high in vitamin C.
4 or more servings

Grain Group
Bread, cereal, rice, pasta.
4 or more servings

Sweets/Fats
No specific amount is recommended. Use in moderation.

Appendix 2
Suggestions for Further Reading

The Annapolis Book of Seamanship, John Rousmaniere. Simon & Schuster (1983). Written for sailors, this very detailed work contains a wealth of vital information.

Boats, Oars & Rowing, R.D. Culler. International Marine Publishing Co. (1978). The title says it all. A collection of wisdom from a master boatbuilder and oarsman. Emphasis on traditional craft.

Building Classic Small Craft (Volumes 1 and 2), John Gardner. International Marine Publishing Co. (1977 and 1984). Full of information, not only on the design and building of classic boats, but also their history and use.

The Dory Book, John Gardner. International Marine Publishing Co. (1978). The definitive work on this classic rowing boat.

The Oxford & Cambridge Boat Race, Christopher Dodd. Stanley Paul (1983). The story of the oldest rowing regatta, packed with history.

Sail and Oar, John Leather. International Marine Publishing Co. (1982). A survey of designs, mostly traditional, some modern.

The Shell Game: Reflections on Rowing and the Pursuit of Excellence, Stephen Kiesling. William Morrow and Company (1982). More on life than on rowing, but an enjoyable, enlightening, introspective look into intercollegiate rowing at the highest level.

A Short History of American Rowing, Thomas Mendenhall. Charles River Books. A lot of statistics and some interesting little-known facts about racing in the United States.

Yacht Cruising, Patrick Ellam. W.W. Norton (1983). A lot of useful information for anyone who ventures offshore.

PERIODICALS

Messing About in Boats, Bob Hicks, 29 Burley St., Wenham, Massachusetts. Published twice monthly. Articles on small-boat rowing and cruising.

Rowing USA, United States Rowing Association, Indianapolis, Indiana. Published bimonthly. Articles on rowing, specifically competitive collegiate and international.

Small Boat Journal, Small Boat Journal, Inc., Bennington, Vermont. Published bimonthly. Articles on the design, construction, and use of rowing boats. Regular boat tests and an Oarlocker column. Considerable information for the do-it-yourselfer.

WoodenBoat, WoodenBoat Publications, Brooklin, Maine. Published bimonthly. Contains articles on design, construction, maintenance, and use of wooden boats (including rowing boats), both traditional and modern.

BOOKS ON NUTRITION

The Athlete's Kitchen, Nancy Clark, M.S., R.D. Van Nostrand Reinhold Company, A CBI Publication (1981).

Eating for Endurance, Ellen Coleman. Rubidoux Printing Company (1980).

Nutrition for Athletes: A Handbook for Coaches, American Alliance for Health, Physical Education, and Recreation (1971).

Nutrition for the Fitness Challenge, The American Heart Association (1983).

Appendix 3   Glossary

Arc. The path of the oar blade during the pull-through.

Back (to). To move the boat backward by turning the face of the blade toward the bow and pushing the handles away from the body.

Blade. The spoon-shaped outboard end of a scull.

Bow. The forward end of a shell or boat.

Bucket (to). To allow the body to come forward too soon on the recovery portion of the stroke.

Buck the oar. To bring the body forward to the oar at the end of the pull-through, rather than bringing the oars to the body.

Button (or *collar*). An adjustable flange placed on the sleeve to prevent the oar from sliding through the oarlock and to set the amount of crossover at the grips.

Catch. The placing of the oar in the water to begin the pull-through.

Clog. A wooden and leather sandal used to hold the foot on the stretcher in some boats.

Cockpit. The area where a sculler sits in the boat.

Crab. An expression used to describe an oar that has become trapped in the water and cannot be released.

Double. A sculling boat rowed by two people.

Drive. The pull-through.

Feather (to). To turn the blade parallel to the surface of the water on the recovery.

Fin. A wood or metal skeg attached to the bottom of the hull to help the boat hold a straight course.

Finish. The portion of the pull-through just before the release.

Foot stretcher. See *stretcher.*

Gate. A bar across the open top of an oarlock.

Grip. The rubber or plastic sleeve over the inboard end of the oar, held by the oarsman.

Handle. See *grip.*

Heel cups. Plastic or metal units for supporting the heels on the stretchers, usually used with clogs or straps.

Height. The distance from the highest portion of the seat to the bottom of the oarlock.

Knife in. To take the catch with the blade under-squared, and therefore drive too deeply into the water.

Layback. The rower's backward (toward the bow) lean at the release, about 15 degrees.

Leather. See *sleeve.*

Oarlock (or *lock*). A U-shaped metal or plastic fitting that holds the oar and swivels around the pin.

Outrigger (or *rigger*). A framework that places the oarlocks outboard of the hull.

Pin (or *tholepin*). A vertical rod attached to the sill, upon which the oarlock swivels.

Pitch. Deviation from the vertical expressed in degrees. In the rower's usual context, the total pitch is the sum of the pitches of the oar and the oarlock.

Port. The left side of the boat when facing the bow.

Puddles. Swirls or disturbances left in the water when the oar is released.

Rate. Number of strokes per minute.

Recovery. The portion of the stroke between release and catch.

Release. The portion of the stroke at which the blade is lifted from the water and feathered.

Rigger. See *outrigger.*

Run (of the boat). The distance the boat travels between the release and the catch.

Scull. To row with a pair of oars.

Sculls. Oars (usually 9 feet, 9 or 10 inches long) used in pairs.

Shaft. The portion of an oar between the blade and grip.

Sill. The plate at the outboard end of the riggers on which the oarlock is mounted.

Single. A sculling boat for one person.

Sleeve (or *leather*). The plastic covering of the oar that prevents wear on the shaft at the oarlock.

Sliding seat. A seat that rolls fore and aft on wheels.

Splay. The angle between the clogs or shoes on the stretcher.

Spread. The distance from pin to pin, measured at their centers.

Starboard. The right side of the boat when facing forward.

Stretcher. An angled plate that provides support for the feet.

Tholepin. See *pin.*

Wash out. To have the blade leave the water before the release.

Index

ARS rowing boats, 9, 14, 15, 17, 18, 26, 107, 110, 114-115, 118, 119, 121
Accessories, 72-73, 105-106, 115, 119
Aero rowing boat, 17, 114, 115, 116, 118, 119, 121
Aerobic exercise, 4, 83
Aesthetics, 23-24
Alden Ocean Shells, 13, 14, 15, 16-17, 19, 62, 118
Aluminum hardware, 21
Anacapa Island, 123, 125-130, 132-134
Anaerobic exercise, 83
Appledore Pod, 9, 11, 14, 16, 19, 24, 25, 29, 110, 124. *See also* Kavienga
Armorall, 72
Arms-only rowing, 96-97

Back splash, 48
Back stretch, 88
Backing, 48-49
Bailing, 23, 72, 79, 106
Balance, 41, 43, 44-46, 53, 63. *See also* Stability
Bat boat, 115
Bay-to-Bay Race, 119
Beam, 13
Bent-over rowing, 89

Better boat, 95-96, 107, 110
Biremes, 2
Boarding, 36-40, 98-99
Boat selection, 6-26
Boatworks, The, 117
Body angle, 47. *See also* Layback position
Boston Whitehall, 16
Bucketing, 58
Bucking the oars, 58
Buttons, 34-35, 67

California Wherry, 9, 10, 17, 107, 110, 114, 115-116, 118
Capsize drill, 81
Capsizing, 80-81
Carbon fiber sculls, 66-67
Carts, 29, 92-93
Catalina 14 rowing boat, 18
Catalina–Marina del Rey Race, 14, 59, 102
Catch position, 43, 51, 62, 88
Chamberlain Dory, 16
Channel Islands. *See* Santa Barbara Channel Islands
Chicken-wing position, 53
Christian Maas Boat Company, 113
Clogs, 72, 105
Clothes, 3, 75-76

Clubs, 25, 96, 101-102, 112-113, 114, 116, 120
Coast Guard, 77, 100
Cockpits, 22-23
Coffey exercise shell, 17
Collars, 34
Collisions, 81-82
Compass, 79, 105, 106
Concept II oars, 115
Construction techniques, 10-12, 19-22
Convertible boats, 18-19
Cool-down drill, 61
Corvettes, 2
Cost, 13, 24, 100
Cruising, 107-111, 121-135
Curl exercise, 90
Cycling, 88

Dead lifts, 89
Decking, 20
Dings, 73-74
Dolphin Rowing Club, 120
Dories, 4, 6, 9, 12, 16, 110
Dory-style rowing, 46, 51
Double-seat rowing boats, 8, 16-17, 18-19
Drills, 45-46, 59-61, 81, 86, 88-90. See *also* Exercises; Stretches
Dromonds, 2

Electronics, 73, 119
Elvstrom bailer, 23
Encounter Pod, 16, 29
Engine bed, 20, 21
Exercises, 83-85. See *also* Drills; Stretches

Fastart rowing boat, 16-17, 20
Feathering, 43, 44, 45, 53-54, 62-63
Fiberglass care, 73-74
Fine-tuning, 56-57, 105
Firefly rowing boat, 16
First row, 40-46
Fisher, Bill, 114
Fixed rigging, 15-18
Fixed-seat rowing, 92
Flashlight, 80
Flexing, 13, 19, 20-21
Float plan, 80, 125
Flotation, 22-23, 125
Fog conditions, 78-79, 134-135
Foot-stretcher arrangements, 3, 21-22, 35-36, 42, 57, 71-72, 81, 105-106

French curl exercise, 90
Front splash, 48

Galleys, 2
Gated oarlock, 21, 33, 34
Gender differences, 42, 92, 94
Gloucester Gull Dory, 16
Graham Mark I, 14, 16-17, 23
Graham rigging unit, 15
Grand Banks dory, 16
Great Cross Sound Race, 102
Grip, 43
Guide boats, 6, 10

Hagerman, Frederick C., 84-85
Half-slide rowing, 61
Hamstring stretch, 87-88
Head coverings, 76
Health benefits, 83-90
Heart rate, 62, 84, 85, 86, 87
History of rowing boats, 1-5
Hoban Kite Wherry, 24
Hulls, 19-20, 73-75
Hull-to-deck joints, 20

Inspection ports, 109
Instruments. *See* Accessories
Intervals, 87

Kavienga (peapod), 124-135
King Fisher racing shell, 17
Kittery Skiff, 16
Knifing in, 46, 55, 57, 58
Knotmeter, 106

File 2 of Index

Lake Tahoe, 117, 119-120
Lake Tahoe North End Rowing Club, 116
Lake Tahoe North Shore Regatta, 102, 116-121
Landing, 41
Laser Shell, 14, 16, 18, 20, 26, 28
Latanzo gated oarlock, 21, 33, 34, 67-68
Latanzo sliding seat, 28, 69-70
Launching, 40
Layback position, 47, 53, 62, 63, 88
Light Hall rowing boat, 17
Lightning rowing boat, 17
Lights, 80
Limitations, 77, 80, 103

Load-carrying ability, 11, 12, 18-19, 110
Lock Tight, 21
Locking oarlocks, 39-40
Long ships, 2
Long-distance rowing, 109, 122. *See also* Cruising
Lubricants, 35, 67, 70

Maas, Christian, 113, 114, 115, 118, 119, 120, 121
Maas 29 rowing boat, 17
Maintenance, 13, 19, 22, 65-76. *See also* Fine-tuning; Tuning
Martin, Arthur, 4, 7, 13, 33, 91
Martin Marine, 7-9, 21, 124
Martin Trainer, 17, 118
Mental set, 51
Military press exercise, 90
Modern pulling boats, 10-26
Modifications, 104-107, 108-109, 124. *See also* Better boat
Monterey Bay rowing boat, 17
Muscles, 56, 89, 90, 93

Nash, Gordie, 14, 26, 59, 107, 113, 114, 115-116, 118, 119, 120, 121
National Park Service, 123
New York Whitehall, 16, 110
No-feather rowing, 45-46, 61
No-leg rowing, 59
Nutrition, 85

Oarlock height, 30-31, 42-43, 57, 69
Oarlock pitch, 31-34, 57, 68
Oarlock pressure plates, 41
Oarlock spread, 13, 34
Oarlocks, 13, 21, 30-34, 39-40, 41, 42-43, 57, 67-68, 69. *See also* Outriggers
Oarmaster, 7-9, 13, 15, 19, 33, 68, 69, 70-71, 124
Oars. *See* Sculls
Oilcanning, 13, 19
Olympics (1984), 91
On Board Rower, 10
Open Water Rowing, 113
Outriggers, 2, 3, 4, 15-18, 20-21, 68-69, 114-115. *See also* Oarmaster
Over-the-hill rowing, 46, 58
Oxford-Cambridge Race (1829), 2

PFD, 79, 124
Pacific Intra-Club Yacht Association Opening Day, 113
Pacific Oars, 113, 115

Pacific 29 rowing boat, 17
Paintedosis oars, 115
Pants, 3, 75
Pause drill, 46, 61
Peapods, 4, 6, 9, 12, 16, 29, 110, 124. *See also* Kavienga
Personal flotation device. *See* PFD
Pitch gauge, 32, 33
Pocock Wherry, 17, 28
Power clean exercise, 89
Pregnancy exercise, 94
Pressure-to-rest ratio, 87
Problems, 46-48, 57-58
Puddles, 61-62
Pulling boats, 6-7, 10-26
Pyramids, 86-87

Quadriremes, 2
Quinqueremes, 2

Racing, 94, 96-107. *See also* Regattas
Racing shell look-alikes, 9, 10-26
Racing shells, 3-4, 6, 7, 12, 17, 98, 99-100
Recovery position, 43, 88
Rec-Racer, 17, 114, 118
Recreational rowing, 3-5, 95-111
Recreational rowing boat, 9-10
Red Cross, 100
Reference points, 64
Regattas, 100-107, 116-121
Removable rigging, 15-18
Rest position, 44
Riggers. *See* Outriggers
Rigging, 15-18. *See also* Outriggers
Righting, 80-81, 99-100
Robinson racing shell, 17
Rollers, 93, 129
Rolling-seat rowing. *See* Sliding-seat rowing
Roll-ups, 63
Roof racks, 27-28, 92
Rough-water ability. *See* Stability
Row Cat, 10
Rowboat rowing, 46
Rowing Crafters, 14, 113, 118
Rowing USA magazine, 84
Rubrails, 20
Running, 88
Running stairs exercise, 88

Safety equipment, 79-80, 124
Safety precautions, 22-23, 77-82, 102-104, 108, 132, 134

Sahure, Pharaoh, 1
Sailing ability, 11
Santa Anas, 125
Santa Barbara Channel Islands, 123-125
Santa Cruz Island, 123, 130-131
Sausalito Rowing Club, 112-113, 114
Schedule, 86
Scull covers, 29, 66
Scull overlap, 35, 44, 57
Scull pitch, 32
Scullcraft, 20
Sculls, 29, 32, 34-35, 44, 57, 66-67, 113, 115, 124
Sea Shell, 14, 16-17
Seat assembly. *See* Sliding-seat assembly
Self-bailers, 23
Seminar, 112-116
Setting course, 63-64
Shoes, 72, 81, 105-106
Shorts, 75-76
Skiffs, 6
Skill level, 25-26. *See also* Limitations
Skying the blades, 47-48, 58
Sleeves, 34, 35, 67
Slide control, 47, 54, 59
Sliding-seat assembly, 21, 28, 36, 69-71, 105
Sliding-seat rowing, 3-5, 7-9, 91
Small Boat Rowing Race, 102
Small Craft, 71, 113, 114, 118
Small Craft Warning, 14, 17, 20, 26, 28, 113, 118
Snatch exercise, 89
Socks, 75
Speed, 13-15, 16-17, 50, 58-59, 63, 87, 110
Spin turn, 49
Splash box, 98, 100
Splashing, 48
Squat exercise, 89
Stability, 4, 11, 12, 13-15, 16-17, 62-64, 110
Starting, 96-97
Steering, 63-64, 97
Stonington Pulling Boat, 9, 11, 14, 16
Stopwatch, 105
Storage, 15-18, 73, 74
Stretches, 87-88. *See also* Drills; Exercises
Stroke length, 46-47, 48
Stroke meter, 106
Stroke pyramid, 86
Stroke rate, 97

Stroke technique, 43, 44, 45, 50-64
Stroke-to-recovery ratio, 44-45, 47, 54, 58-59
Suction-style bailer, 72, 106
Super Seat, 71
Swampscott dory, 11, 16
Swimming, 77, 88

Tapping, 45, 47, 58
Thompson, Peter, 116, 119, 121
Tights, 75
Time pyramid, 86
Timing devices, 105, 106
Track assembly. *See* Sliding-seat assembly
Traditional craft imitators, 9, 10-26
Trailers, 29
Trainers, 97-99
Transporting, 27-29, 92-93, 129
Triple-seat rowing boats, 16-17
Triremes, 2
Tuning up, 29-36
Turning, 48-49
22-minute drill, 88-90

Unadjustable oarlocks, 21, 33
Uncontrolled slide, 47
Use, 24-26

Vancouver 21 rowing boat, 9, 14, 17, 25, 26, 107, 110, 114, 115, 116, 118, 119
Vanderruden, 109
Velcro straps, 72, 105
Viking 22 rowing boat, 16-17
Viking Whitehall, 9

WEST System, 11, 24, 73, 74
Warships, 2
Watches, 105
Water conditions, 78-79, 103
Water-bottle mounts, 105
Weather conditions, 62-64, 103, 125. *See also* Fog conditions
Weight-lifting, 88-90
Whaleboats, 2
Whitehalls, 4, 6, 9, 10, 11, 12, 16, 110
Wind conditions, 63, 125
Wings, 114-115
Women rowers, 91-94
Wood protection, 72
Wooden sculls, 66-67
Workboats, 4, 6
Workouts, 85-87

Yale-Harvard Race (1852), 2-3